Victoria Woodhull

Free Spirit for Women's Rights

OXFORD
PORTRAITS

Victoria Woodhull

Free Spirit for Women's Rights

Miriam Brody

OXFORD
UNIVERSITY PRESS

With love and welcome to Samuel Oscar Lawrence Kramnick—already vocal, eloquent, and a passionate advocate.

OXFORD
UNIVERSITY PRESS

Oxford   New York
Auckland   Bangkok   Buenos Aires   Cape Town   Chennai
Dar es Salaam   Delhi   Hong Kong   Istanbul   Karachi   Kolkata
Kuala Lumpur   Madrid   Melbourne   Mexico City   Mumbai   Nairobi
São Paulo   Shanghai   Taipei   Tokyo   Toronto

Copyright © 2003 by Miriam Brody

Published by Oxford University Press, Inc.
198 Madison Avenue, New York, New York 10016
www.oup.com

Oxford is a registered trademark of Oxford University Press

Design and layout: Greg Wozney
Picture research: Ted Szczepanski

Library of Congress Cataloging-in-Publication Data
Brody, Miriam
Victoria Woodhull : free spirit for women's rights / Miriam Brody.
v. cm. — (Oxford portraits)
Includes bibliographical references and index.
Contents: The Claflins, the Woodhulls, and the Spiritual Telegraph —
Gotham : broker, candidate, and journalist — Taking up the burden : the
petitioner for woman suffrage — Rocking the boat : the "social questions" —
Parting the Red Sea : on the campaign trail — Standing alone : Woodhull under
attack? Safe harbor : the second career of Victoria Woodhull.
ISBN 0-19-514367-1 (alk. paper)
1. Woodhull, Victoria C. (Victoria Claflin), 1838-1927 — Juvenile literature.
2. Feminists — United States — Biography — Juvenile literature. 3. Suffragists —
United States — Biography — Juvenile literature. 4. Women in politics —
United States — Biography — Juvenile literature. [1. Woodhull, Victoria C.
(Victoria Claflin), 1838–1927. 2. Feminists. 3. Presidential candidates.
4. Women — Biography.] I. Title. II. Series.

HQ1413.W66B76 2003
305.42'092--dc22[B]

2003024161

9 8 7 6 5 4 3 2 1

Printed in the United States of America on acid-free paper

On the cover: Victoria Woodhull, about 1885
Frontispiece: Victoria Woodhull, about 1871

CONTENTS

PREFACE: NEW YORK CITY, NOVEMBER 5, 1872

Election day passed quietly. By noon the air was springlike, and it stayed warm into evening, long after the polls had closed. More surprising, the city was almost peaceful, not as rowdy as it often was on election days. Uptown at the Astor Hotel on Fifth Avenue, crowds waited to hear how the *New York Tribune*'s editor, Horace Greeley, had fared against President Ulysses S. Grant. But no bonfires were lit. No property was looted. Nor was there much speculation about the chances of another Presidential candidate, the first woman ever to be nominated for such a high office. She was a woman of striking beauty and spellbinding dramatic presence, someone who was lending a powerful voice to the most radical reforms of her time. On this election day the notorious and outspoken Victoria Woodhull was in jail. She had been arrested the day before, accosted by police officers at her place of business as though she were a common criminal.

The downfall of Victoria Woodhull was as swift as her climb to prominence. Only a few years earlier, she had come to New York City from the Midwest, bringing with her a gift for oratory and an abiding belief in the greatness of her own destiny. She had learned firsthand the harsh deprivations of poverty on the American frontier. She also knew the desperate powerlessness of many women, whose economic and political dependency was supported by longstanding legal and social tradition. Determined to forge her own independence, she became a financier—the first woman to open a brokerage house on Wall Street—and then a muckraking publisher, uncovering corruption among the new industrialists who were transforming the United States from a rural economy into a great manufacturing nation.

In speeches that captured headlines, Woodhull demanded economic reforms to relieve the poverty of the new laboring classes crowding into the cities since the Civil War had ended. She helped to revitalize the woman suffrage movement by calling on women to storm polling places and insist upon their right to vote. Bravely challenging the social taboos of her time, she urged educational reforms that would release women from the sexual ignorance that generated not only unhappiness but disease and death. She became a figure of astounding controversy, considered by some to be so dangerous she was called "Mrs. Satan." Standing in the closing decades of the 19th century, Victoria Woodhull became a spokesperson for grievances that would engage activists far into the next century.

Those who sympathized with the outcast "Mrs. Satan" would have to wait a long time for her vindication. In the course of her campaign for humanitarian reforms she made many powerful enemies. On election day in 1872, the day when she had hoped to witness her triumph, the campaign to silence and disarm her had only begun.

THE CLAFLINS, THE WOODHULLS, AND THE SPIRITUAL TELEGRAPH

Such another family-circle of cats and kits, with soft fur and sharp claws, purring at one moment and fighting the next, never before filled one house with their clamors since Babel began.

—Theodore Tilton, *Victoria C. Woodhull, A Biographical Sketch*

Late in the third decade of the 19th century, Reuben Buckman Claflin, hoping to make his fortune, brought his young family to a small out-of-the-way hamlet in the grass-lands of Ohio. Buck Claflin was the kind of rough-shod American the times favored. An able man, quick of speech, a daredevil, and a hard drinker, he was a man on the make when the century was young. To be sure, not all young people could hope for so much fortune as could Buck. It was a time when most Americans still supported what the South called their "peculiar institution" of slavery, a time when federal policy was driving Native Americans from their lands, a time when women were legally under the control of the men they had married. But if the fortune-seeker were a young white man, like Buck Claflin, then America was rich with promise. In the northeastern states, railroad tracks were being laid, and land values climbed. In the north central states, speculation in land was equally fruitful. If eastern farmland or cities such as Boston, New York, or Richmond ceased to please, a man could move west and start over.

With the opening of New York's Erie Canal in 1825, trade opportunities beckoned in Ohio—a chance for riches to which Buck Claflin responded. At first he may have had genteel pretensions. He had studied a little law as a youth and could find his way around a courtroom if anyone wanted to bring a lawsuit against a neighbor. But by the time Buck reached the Pennsylvania towns along the banks of the Susquehanna River, he had learned to be a horse trader among the river swindlers, passing off a team of slick-looking horses before the paint on them wore away. He knew how to cut a deck of cards and remember where each card lay. He was tall and slender with a big beak of a nose, and by the time youth had passed, his character was stamped on his face. "He looked like a sneak," said anarchist publisher Benjamin Tucker, who met him years later, "and a skinflint."

In Pennsylvania in 1825 Buck met and married Roxanna "Annie" Hummel, whose German father kept a tavern, and whose flashes of temper and ready tongue equaled Buck's. Although, like most poor people in the country, Annie could neither read nor write, she claimed a special kind of intelligence, an ability to commune with spirits, for which no book learning was necessary. Seeking religious salvation, Annie had found her way to the camp meetings that preachers were setting up all over the countryside in a movement of such religious fervor it recalled the "Great Awakening" revival of a century earlier.

These evangelical preachers offered passionate sermons to the new settlers, some still living in the wagons they had

Victoria Woodhull's father, Reuben "Buck" Claflin, was a hustler, con artist, and blackmailer who exploited his young daughters for ready cash. Yet when Woodhull needed to display a more respectable parent, she called him "the most noble" and "the wisest of counselors."

Revivalist meetings where traveling preachers encouraged the faithful to accept salvation were popular along the American frontier. Poor, uneducated women like Victoria Woodhull's mother, were enthusiastic participants at such meetings.

used to cross the plains. The Methodist preachers to whom Annie was drawn described a powerful god who separated the saved from the damned and consigned sinners to the torments of eternal hellfire. Annie often walked at twilight toward the bonfires and the trumpet blasts of the camp meetings, hoping for God's grace. With tears of religious ecstasy she embraced salvation so joyously that she fell to the ground in a trance calling out "Hallelujah!" When she stood in her yard and babbled in the voices of her mystical visions, she wept and cried out. Foam sometimes settled on her lips. Her neighbors thought she was mad.

Annie's religious passion was a mixed brew all her own. To the sermons of the campground Methodists she added the simple superstitions of a barely educated country girl, superstitions that found fertile ground in her nature. Her religious frenzies may also have been fed by both mental instability and some talent for dramatic outbursts. Annie believed that when she was in a trance and babbling incoherently God was speaking through her in a divine, apparently incomprehensible language. Her belief in speaking in tongues, scorned by the neighbors, became common practice in the Pentecostal religious movement in the twentieth century. But when she claimed to hear the voices of the dead, or believed that others did, she was in advance of a growing new religion called "spiritualism."

By the middle of the 19th century, a belief in the existence of spirits was taking shape across America as a separate religious identity. By communicating with the dead, spiritualists sought to prove the immortality of the soul and the existence of an afterlife, a quest that served many purposes. Some spiritualists sought entertainment; some who grieved the loss of loved ones sought solace; many others searched for a new grounding of religious faith. Annie's faith, part theater, part hokum, part religious conviction, anticipated spiritualism and offered a legacy her children learned to value and to use.

The eccentric and unstable Roxanna "Annie" Hummel Claflin embarrassed and harassed her daughter Victoria, while still eliciting her loyalty. "Our blessed angel," Woodhull called her mother after her death.

With Annie and a growing family, Buck Claflin came to Homer, Ohio, a farming town of a just a few hundred people, forty miles northeast of Columbus. He bought a grist mill where villagers could bring their grain to be ground into flour, and moved his family into a ramshackle homestead, which Annie Claflin, lost in religious reveries, kept poorly. Even had she been more willing, housekeeping was not easy in pre–Civil War America. Water for cooking, drinking, and washing had to be collected in rainwater cisterns or hauled from streams or backyard wells. Too often the wells were placed near the backyard privy, and sewage-borne diseases flourished. When it rained, it was easy to track in mud from the unpaved streets, filthy from the refuse in the flooded ditches. Children were especially vulnerable to plagues of cholera, malaria, and typhus.

The Claflins' seventh child and third living daughter, Victoria, was born in 1838 and named after the young queen of England, crowned a year earlier in London. Much of what we know about Victoria Woodhull's childhood is derived from an account she related years later to Theodore Tilton, one of post–Civil War America's leading intellectuals, who wrote a short biographical essay about her. Hers, she told Tilton, was a childhood scarred by harsh treatment and spent in hard work. She worked like "a little steam engine," making fires, washing, ironing, baking bread, cutting wood, tending the vegetable garden, and taking care of two younger sisters. She claimed to have been a favorite in the neighborhood, a beautiful and graceful child. But in her own family, as Theodore Tilton recorded, she was worked "like a slave" and whipped "like a convict."

Victoria's father, wrote Tilton, was "impartial in his cruelty to all his children." "In a barrel of rain-water," he wrote, "he kept a number of braided green switches, made of willow or walnut twigs, and with these stinging weapons, never with an ordinary whip, he would cut the quivering flesh of his children till their tears and blood melted him into mercy." "I have no remembrance of a father's kiss," Woodhull told Tilton, "only his blows."

Woodhull told Tilton that Annie occasionally defended her children, but she was just as likely to add her own torments and harassment. One moment she would be angelic, cuddling her babies, weeping over them, lifting her arms to thank God for her children and caressing them with "ecstatic joy." The next moment she might strike them herself, "as if seeking to destroy at a blow both body and soul." Looking, wrote Tilton, "as fiercely delighted as a cat play-

SISTERHOOD OF FURIES

The abolitionist and reformer Theodore Tilton wrote a biographical sketch of Victoria Woodhull in 1871. To woo the spiritualists, whose support Woodhull was seeking for her Presidential campaign, Tilton's narrative pamphlet dwelt dramatically on Woodhull's childhood clairvoyant experiences. In this passage, however, he reserves the melodrama for a description of the incomparable Claflin family of fortune-tellers, blackmailers, and hysterics.

It is pitiful to be a child without a childhood. Such was she. Not a sunbeam gilded the morning of her life. Her girlish career was a continuous bitterness—an unbroken heart-break. She was worked like a slave—whipped like a convict. . . . At times, they [Woodhull's parents] are full of craftiness, low cunning, and malevolence; at other times, they beam with sunshine, sweetness, and sincerity. I have seen many strange people, but the strangest of all are the two parents whose commingled essence constitutes the spiritual principle of the heroine of this tale. Just here, if any one asks, "How is it that such parents should not have reproduced their eccentricities in their children?" I answer, "This is exactly what they have done." The whole brood are of the same feather—except Victoria and Tennie. What language shall describe them? . . . They love and hate—they do good and evil—they bless and smite each other. They are a sisterhood of furies, tempered with love's melancholy. Here and there one will drop on her knees and invoke God's vengeance on the rest. But for years there has been one common sentiment sweetly pervading the breasts of a majority towards a minority of the offspring, namely a determination that Victoria and Tennie should earn all the money for the support of the numerous remainder of the Claflin tribe—wives, husbands, children, servants, and all. Being daughters of the horseleech, they cry "give." It is the common law of the Claflin clan that the idle many shall eat up the substance of the thrifty few . . . They are . . . "a bad crowd."

ing with a mouse," when her children wept she clapped her hands and laughed "hysterically."

Buck's temper was not improved by the failure of his land-speculation schemes. To his daughter, Tilton wrote, it seemed that he simply "sat down like a beggar in the dust of despair." Whatever hopes had buoyed him as a young man on the banks of the Susquehanna, by the time his numerous children were clambering over the rough planks of the porch in Homer, Buck had given up. Sometimes he simply disappeared, wrote Tilton, and would return home after long walks with "bleeding feet and a haggard face." Then Annie would "huddle her children together as a hen her chickens, and wringing her hands above them, would pray by the hour that God would protect her little brood."

The Claflin children learned to depend on themselves. Like most children in the frontier states, they spent little time in a schoolhouse. With only three years at school, Victoria Claflin had no more formal education than Abraham Lincoln had received ten years earlier on the Indiana frontier. What education she had was hard won, shaped more by Buck and Annie than by schoolteachers. From her father, she learned she could rely on no one. Disaster, whether from poverty or abuse, could be sudden and crushing. If she were to survive, it must be by the exercise of her own wits. From her mother, she learned that help might as easily come from the spirit world as from a neighbor or a friend.

As a child, Victoria often trailed after her mother to the evening campground revival meetings, where she sat spellbound under the tent. In the magical glow of firelight, Victoria absorbed the rhythms of the evangelical sermons as easily as she breathed in the scent of the windswept high grasses. Beside her Annie swayed and moaned in joyous communion with spirits. Rocked by her mother into religious ecstasy, Victoria felt possessed of something invisible and powerful. As she told the story later to Theodore

Tilton, one night, returning from a camp meeting with her mother, she cried out "Mamma, stop to hear voices." The voices, she said to her mother, were warning her that men would rob their house that night; to prevent them, they must light all the lamps. Impressed, Annie did. The robbers came the next day, said Victoria, and they went away. There was no one to prove her wrong.

Another day, when she was 10 years old and left to tend her sick baby sister in her cradle, Victoria fell asleep. When her mother came home and might have been angry, Victoria told her that angels had put her in a trance and fanned the feverish baby with their own white hands. The baby, she announced, was not feverish any longer. Annie, by now convinced that Victoria was blessed indeed with mystical powers, clasped her daughter joyously to her. Resilient and resourceful, little Vicky Claflin created her own world of voices and visions that counseled and defended her. There was no other means of escape. She could not simply run away from home, as one of her brothers did at thirteen. How would she live? Yet when she was not so much older than her brother, a very real means of escape did present itself, one that the spirits did not provide.

Victoria Claflin met the man who would become her husband when she was still a girl of fourteen. Catastrophe had ended the Claflin family business in Homer. A gas lamp overturned in Buck's grist mill, and the dry grain burst into flames. The bucket brigade organized hastily by neighbors could do little to stop the blaze, and before the evening had passed, the mill was reduced to ashes. With Buck out of town, Annie gathered her children to her, wringing her hands in despair and weeping to the heavens for mercy. The neighbors clucked sympathetically at the Claflins' misfortune, but no one trusted Buck Claflin. If he had not set the fire for the insurance money, surely he wished he had.

In the early 1850s, with property values dropping in an economic downturn, the Claflins were not the only family worrying about their losses. Most people in Ohio shared a general sense of disappointment that the riches promised by the opening of the Erie Canal in 1825 were not so dependable. The neighbors took up a collection, and, their meager belongings stashed into wagons, Buck, Annie, and the children left for Mt. Gilead, a small town west of Homer where Maggie, their married eldest daughter, lived.

When the Claflins moved to Mt. Gilead, Victoria was not feeling well. The long damp winters had seemed to settle in her bones, and for many months she could not shake an aching rheumatism, often worsened by chills and fevers. Concerned for her, Annie and Buck called in a young doctor, new to town. Canning Woodhull, 28 years old and good-looking, made a favorable impression, and if he called himself a doctor after only a few months of reading medical books, no one particularly expected otherwise. The infant medical profession had not yet set standards for medical practice.

Whatever ointments or rubdowns the new doctor recommended for a cure, Victoria felt better as the weather changed. As Victoria recalled the scene later for Theodore Tilton, one summer day when she passed Dr. Woodhull on the street, he looked her up and down and said, "My little chick, I want you to go with me to the picnic." The invitation was appealing to a young girl crowded with her family into a small hotel managed by her sister's husband. The outing Dr. Woodhull was proposing was to the village celebration of the Fourth of July.

Telling the story later to Tilton, Victoria imagined herself as a Cinderella, "a child of the ashes," and Dr. Woodhull as the prince. On the way home from the picnic, the doctor announced to Victoria, "My little puss, tell your father and mother that I want you for a wife." Buck and Annie were "delighted at the unexpected offer," remembered Victoria. They thought it a great match, because the doctor was apparently well connected to family back East. As one son-in-law had already conveniently offered the

Claflins a refuge in Mt. Gilead, another son-in-law like Canning Woodhull might provide better, should the need arise. Victoria was still only 14, "ignorant, innocent, and simple," as she described herself later to Tilton. If she knew nothing about the man proposing to make her a home, she did know that she would be leaving no home at all. To be a wife to this handsome doctor would surely be better than to be a daughter to the feckless and brutal Buck.

When Victoria Claflin married Canning Woodhull in 1853, four months after the fateful picnic at Mt. Gilead, she

Victoria and Canning Woodhull with their children, Byron and Zulu, posed for a deceptively peaceful family portrait about 1864, shortly before Woodhull sued Canning for a divorce.

became almost invisible in the eyes of the law, which considered a married couple to be one person—and that person the husband. English common law, which formed the basis for American law, denied married women the right to control their own money. Just as a "small brooke" or "rivulet" loses its name when it is carried away by a more powerful river, so too, explained English common law, a woman as soon as she is married is "clouded and overshadowed. . . ." "To a married woman, her new self is her superior, her companion, her master."

When she married, it was as though, legally, the person of Victoria Claflin had ceased to be. As a wife, she would have no right to resist her husband beating her as long as the beating was "reasonable," no right to deny him sexual relations, nor any right to claim that the children of her marriage belonged as much to her as to her husband. To be sure, by the mid-19th century most states had begun to pass legislation to entitle married women to retain property. The new American Republic prized hard work, independence, and entitlement to all the riches and privileges one could make the new land yield. But the tradition and practice that resisted these reforms were longstanding and deeply rooted.

When she was barely 15 years old, Victoria Claflin became Victoria Woodhull in a simple civil ceremony in Cleveland. Only days later she discovered that her new husband was no Prince Charming after all. Canning Woodhull was, in fact, a drunk and a libertine, with few ties to his more fortunate family back East, who seemed to regard him as a castoff. Four days after becoming his bride, Victoria lay awake all night waiting for her husband to return from an evening's drinking. As she waited, the young girl realized how perilous her marriage was to this man she barely knew. She told Tilton that she was "stung to the quick" and "grew ten years older in a single day."

Her first response to misfortune was like her mother's would have been. She wept and prayed, calling on spirits to help her reform the man to whom she had so unwittingly tied herself. But Canning Woodhull was beyond appeal to reform. While Victoria spent wretched nights watching for him from the window of the simple rooms he rented for her, Canning sought out the women in the town who were willing to entertain him for a fee, while he played the dashing playboy who ordered baskets of champagne. Still a young girl herself, Victoria Woodhull was left to call upon her own resources. She had been, she told Tilton, "a child without a childhood." That child was now irretrievably an adult, tied to a diseased and dissolute man who would never earn money as a doctor, and who indeed showed little interest in trying.

Many years later she printed memories of the promising bachelor Canning Woodhull in her newspaper, *Woodhull & Claflin's Weekly,* recalling that the doctor from a good family had seemed such "a desirable match." Describing the illusions of girlhood, she wrote "I supposed that to marry was to be transported to a heaven not only of happiness but of purity and perfection. . . . I believed it to be the one good thing there was on the earth and that a husband must necessarily be an angel, impossible of corruption or contamination." The young girl who had believed such dreams now vanished forever. Expecting her first child, Victoria waited out her baby's birth in unheated rooms, while her husband caroused in nearby taverns. She would forever deny that love and marriage were two sides of the same coin.

Never in one place very long, Victoria and Canning Woodhull were living in a low frame house in Chicago when their son Byron was born, a little more than a year after their marriage. Victoria remembered that icicles clung to her bedframe, and that she would have died from neglect after the baby was born if a kind neighbor and her own mother had not arrived to help. Taking stock of the dismal surroundings, Annie Claflin bundled up her daughter and new grandson and took them home with her to recover.

Meanwhile, Canning Woodhull's revelries moved from nearby taverns into their own rooms. Victoria returned to Chicago to find their apartment in disarray and littered with the remains of a drunken feast. Worse discoveries lay in wait. The infant Byron was not developing as a baby should. To her great sorrow, Victoria realized that her baby was seriously impaired—a "half idiot," she said to Tilton, as doctors of her time would have described him. "Begotten in drunkenness and born in squalor," wrote Tilton, the poor boy would never learn to speak nor to care for himself. Woodhull was convinced that Canning's alcoholism resulted in his son's retardation. She still clung to a naive belief that only a man and a woman truly in love could produce a healthy child. Sadly, no true love had attended the conception of this son. Instead, Canning Woodhull, whom Victoria soon discovered to be an unrepentant drunk, repelled his young bride. Slowly, Victoria grew to understand that Canning would be no more fit as a father to his son than he was as a husband to his wife.

At sixteen, Victoria Woodhull found herself mother of a son who would never grow up and wife to a man who, grown up, was no better than a child. She might easily have sat down in the dust of her despair, as she recalled her father doing. But something resilient in Victoria Woodhull prevailed. Though she spoke to later audiences about her childhood belief that marriage promised a fairy tale happiness for women, nothing in her parents' household could have been the model for such an illusion. She had not been raised on daydreams, but on hard work and the conviction that good fortune fell to the person who pursued it. With Canning seldom sober, and a child to feed, Woodhull became the manager of her family's destiny. Like so many before her, she migrated west.

When Victoria was still a child, the flash of gold dust in the streambeds of California had sent prospectors westward in wagons to make their fortunes, settling into mining camps with names like Red Dog, Grub Gulch, or Poker Flat. Farmers, clerks, ministers, and pioneers who had not yet cleared their land caught gold-rush fever and packed up to stake a claim and "get rich quick." Victoria Woodhull was young and healthy, and though burdened with an alcoholic husband and a needy child, she arranged to move with her family to San Francisco, where something better might be waiting.

By the time she arrived in San Francisco with Canning and Byron, a half-dozen years after the first gold strike, that muddy little village had become a city, with gaslights, cobblestones in the streets, and old timber houses replaced with brick. California, growing rapidly, boasted a governor and a legislature and was proudly calling itself a state. Dreams of fabulous wealth had faded, but San Francisco, with its noisy dance-hall saloons and dank waterfront rooming houses, had not completely outgrown its rough and ready beginnings. A fortune in gold found the night before might still trade hands in a card game at the gambling palaces along the waterfront, where Indians, Chinese, French, and Englishmen jostled Hoosiers from Indiana, Georgia "crackers," and Yankees from New England.

Victoria Woodhull hoped that the contagion of gold-rush fever would somehow awaken in her lackluster husband a new resolve to support his family. The new state would need doctors, even ones with limited training. But as Tilton wrote, "change of sky is not change of mind." The doctor took his old habits with him to California, and the Woodhulls unpacked their familiar misery along with their few belongings. Victoria's family's fortunes would depend on her alone.

Having seen an advertisement in a morning journal for a "cigar girl," Victoria presented herself to the shopkeeper who, after looking her over, gave her a day's trial. All the Claflin daughters were beautiful, a legacy from Buck and Annie that their daughters would trade for useful coin on

Woodhull's sister, Tennessee Claflin, enjoyed startling newspaper readers by being photographed in men's clothing and sporting a boyish haircut. She complained that office life was made difficult by 19th-century women's fashions, which required about 15 pounds of awkward, billowing skirt.

the rough roads they traveled. But, as Theodore Tilton later recorded, Victoria hated the jibes and insults of her customers, who were teasing or simply lewd. "Salty talk," she described it to Tilton, as you might expect from sailors. The proprietor, Tilton wrote, expected his cigar girls to amuse his customers, and told her at day's end, "you are not the clerk I want. I must have somebody who can rough it. You are too fine." The proprietor gave Woodhull a twenty-dollar gold piece and wished her good luck.

In retelling this story later for Tilton, Woodhull drew a refined and demure picture of her younger self, one that seems at odds with the kind of person who could survive the slapdash, hard-edged, makeshift streets of gold-rush San Francisco. But others confirm her surprising gentility, so uncharacteristic of the Claflins, so unlike, for example, her flirtatious younger sister Tennessee, with whom she was often compared. Years later, Benjamin Tucker, the reformer and publisher, remembered this refinement, recalling how she cringed with aversion when her sister Tennessee used coarse language or reached for a bottle of whiskey.

Perhaps Victoria Woodhull did color her narratives of her younger years in San Francisco so as not to startle the sensibilities of the more conventional audiences, whose admiration she sought. It is as likely, however, that the cigar-store proprietor recognized in Woodhull the same refinement that Benjamin Tucker described. A cigar girl who recoiled at "salty talk" would not do. Nor could a penniless young mother with an improvident husband easily find honest work that would feed her family. She barely had skills enough to teach school, work that offered little money anyway. If she were to honor the stiff notions of respectability that the times demanded of women, her family must go hungry.

For a time she plied her needle, trying to earn her way as a seamstress. By chance she met an actress, Anna Cogswell, who hired her to work on costumes for the theater. A seamstress working without a sewing machine might earn as little as $3.00 a week, eye-straining and tedious work with which to remain poor. When she complained to Cogswell that she was falling behind and must find something better, her friend suggested that Woodhull should go on stage herself. The suggestion was not absurd. The theater of the revival tents was a fresh memory. Moreover, since childhood Woodhull had felt she was the conduit for spirit voices. It would not be strange to speak lines in other voices on stage.

Handed a script in the morning, Woodhull learned her lines easily, and, as her actress friend had guessed, the pretty young woman with the strong and pleasant speaking voice was a success on stage. For a month and a half, she earned $52.00 a week as an actress, excellent wages as long as the work held out. The most skilled manual laborer might earn only $15 a week. Woodhull told Tilton she was encouraged to remain an actress. As Tilton recorded the scene, other performers who admired the newcomer's work said, "Never leave the stage," to which Woodhull responded, "but I do not care for the stage, and I shall leave it at the first opportunity. I am meant for some other fate. But what it is, I know not." Woodhull recalled this grand prophecy for Tilton years later, in a memory perhaps more contrived than accurate. But some dissatisfaction with her life on stage or in San Francisco was growing in Victoria Woodhull. She was a young mother in a strange city, with no one near her to depend upon. She was ready to go home, despite the good wages.

The story Woodhull passed on to Theodore Tilton was itself fine theater. She said that one night while she performed onstage, it seemed to her that her sister Tennessee was beckoning to her and saying "Victoria come home." Feeling "thrilled and chilled" by the vision and voice, Woodhull rushed out in her costume into the damp San Francisco fog to make plans to go home. With the money earned onstage, she booked passage for her family on a steamer to New York, an expensive journey that exhausted her earnings. A steerage ticket from the Golden Gate through the Isthmus of Panama was costly. For less money, they might have returned home by land across the mountains and the plains, but the journey would have been more hazardous and lengthy. All too often, wagons broke down and dwindling supplies were exhausted. The Woodhulls had come to California, Tilton wrote, "beggars in a land of plenty." Leaving there would beggar them again. Still, Victoria Woodhull had found riches of a sort in her own compelling and pleasant stage voice. She lacked only something to say. With her marriage hopelessly failed, and her profoundly damaged son poisoned before birth, she believed, by his father's addiction to alcohol, life was providing her with the words she would one day speak.

Meanwhile, Buck Claflin, speculator, grist-mill operator, scoundrel, snake-oil salesman, was spending his middle years managing a family road show of mystics, healers, and fortune-tellers. While his daughter Victoria was

"Buck" Claflin's patent medicine, named for his daughter Tennessee, was a harmless brew, but after one gravely-ill client died in Illinois, Tennessee was indicted for manslaughter and the family hastily fled the state.

making her way home from California, his star was her younger sister Tennessee. Buck would roll into towns across the Midwest with Tennie, claiming in advance billing that she was his "wonderful child." For a dollar a consultation, Tennie could tell a man who his future wife would be, or could receive messages from the dead. She claimed to heal fever sores, cancers, backaches, and sprains with her "Magnetio Life Elixir," a harmless enough brew that Buck compounded from vegetable oil.

By all accounts, Tennie was making a good living. Even at just a dollar a client, she might earn as much as $50 or $100 a day, so long as the sheriff did not run the Claflins out of town. But when Victoria Woodhull descended upon her mother and sister in their hotel rooms in Columbus, Ohio, she found the arrangement unsavory. Her parents were too willing to live off the earnings of their daughter, who at 14 was rapidly becoming more woman than "wonderful child." At a similar age, Victoria had been packed off into a marriage that had proved disastrous.

Not that Victoria Woodhull doubted that her sister had some powers as a healer or as someone who could hear spirit voices. Both Woodhull and Tennie had spent their childhood learning that they could win their mother's love best by communing with spirits. Listening for such voices was natural to them. Woodhull took as a certainty that some human beings, herself and her sister Tennessee among them, were endowed with special powers with which to cure illness and transmit messages from the dead. But Woodhull also believed that her parents were exploiting Tennessee's gifts and would continue to do so as long as they could. As Theodore Tilton wrote later, Buck and Annie were determined that Tennie, and now Victoria, since she had returned to them, should earn all the money "for the support of the numerous remainder of the Claflin tribe."

With her own family to support, Woodhull cast a skeptical eye over the Claflin road show and a wary eye on her sister Tennessee, and joined the Claflin family business. From Ohio, she took her talents to Indiana, where she advertised herself as a clairvoyant, someone who could "see clearly" a client's past or future. She was successful, and began earning money again as she had in San Francisco. She told Tilton that she stitched into the sleeve of her dress a prayer against the temptation to practice fraud: "Deliver my soul O Lord from lying lips and from a deceitful tongue." Yet deliverance from the practice of deception may not have been at hand, for these were hard years, and there were many mouths to feed.

Buck trained his daughters to be good listeners, and many clients were willing to open their purses for the privilege of holding hands with the sympathetic and beautiful Claflin sisters, who issued prophecies and dispensed healing. If Woodhull practiced hokum as a clairvoyant, she may have believed she did no more harm than she had reciting lines on stage. But her younger sister was in clearer danger, being stage managed by the unscrupulous Buck Claflin. One disappointed client of Tennie's took her to court when the "Magnetio Life Elixir" failed to cure. Elsewhere, she was accused of prostitution. Woodhull told Tilton later that her parents mixed "charlatanry with much that was genuine" when they promoted Tennie. By "much that was genuine," Victoria Woodhull meant the spirit world, intangible but to her wholly real.

When she communed with spirits, Woodhull lay claim to powers she had long felt inseparable from her best self. At the same time she became part of a growing number of working women who, excluded from most opportunities for employment, found they could earn good money as "mediums," persons through whom spirits spoke. While the Claflins were taking their road show through the Midwest, a passion for communicating with spirits had long been spreading in the northern and eastern states, set in motion by the experiences of people like the Fox sisters.

Some years earlier, in a farmhouse in the small town of Hydeville, New York, near Rochester, 12- and 14-year-old Margaret and Kate Fox heard sounds for which they could make no account. When the girls rapped on tables and walls, the sounds seemed to respond. Soon Hydesville neighbors crowded into the farmhouse to hear the rapping sounds on walls and furniture. When they asked questions of what they took to be a spirit presence, they learned he had been a peddler, murdered and buried in the cellar.

The Fox sisters' "Rochester rappings" became famous. When one of the Fox sisters sought shelter from the furor by joining an older sister in Rochester, she attracted the interest of a sophisticated, reform-minded community of people, including the respected abolitionist William Lloyd Garrison, who came frequently to Rochester to lecture. Many educated people of the time believed in spirits, including Sarah Grimké, the southern women's rights advocate and abolitionist, and Isabella Beecher Hooker, one of the talented Beecher family of ministers and writers. Mary Todd Lincoln invited mediums to the White House so she could communicate with her dead boy, Willie.

Suddenly everyone was talking about the spirit world, the Fox sisters, and the meetings called séances where they received their messages if conditions were favorable. It was not odd that even well-educated people in the mid-19th century were willing to believe that strange noises were messages from the dead. At a time when so many small children died, parents such as Mary Todd Lincoln longed to believe that their babies were living in paradise. Evangelical ministers were peddling a stern form of the Protestant religion known as Calvinism that spread anguish with its unforgiving doctrine of unbaptized babies' suffering hellfire. Now mediums could translate rappings as reassuring messages from happy children. At one such session, for example, mediums claimed to hear the spirit of a dead two-year-old telling her parents that she was playing with cousins in heaven and would soon be learning to read. Mothers who had lost sons in the Civil War sought out mediums who could bring them reassurance that their sons lived on in heaven. Spiritualism suited midcentury America's optimistic and compassionate conviction that a loving God would reward any deserving American's hard work with heavenly bliss, as well as offer paradise to those who fell on battlefields and comfort to innocent babies who died before baptism.

Spiritualism also promised a new grounding of religious faith in observation of the material world, the only form of proof the age of science valued. Mediums would demonstrate with observable phenomena that the soul lived on after death. Perhaps a table would seem to rise from the floor, or a bouquet of lilies drop from the ceiling. Mysterious noises might emanate from behind the walls, and finally the medium, in a trance, would translate as someone's relative spoke from heaven.

To be sure, more than a few people suspected fraud. Many regarded the mediums and clairvoyants as simply another form of entertainment, to be huckstered and advertised with the enthusiasm of circus showman P. T. Barnum, who brought the Fox sisters to New York City. But to others, spirits speaking through mediums seemed no more improbable than messages traveling across electric wires. In 1842, only a few years before the Fox sisters heard strange rappings, Samuel B. Morse was barely able to convince the Congress of the United States to fund his experimental telegraph line between Washington and Baltimore—few people understood the science on which the telegraph was based. Mediums called their messages the "spiritual telegraph," and the comparison seemed apt.

Many years later, when they were old women, the Fox sisters offered other explanations for their rappings: the peculiar creaking of their toe joints, augmented by servants hired to rap on cellar walls. But by that time spiritualism had done its important work, consoling grieving mothers, entertaining many, and offering up a religious faith based on observing the real world, as science required. Spiritualism rejected old-time Calvinist religion and its belief that only a few could enter heaven, and preached that salvation was possible for everyone. Moreover, spiritualism was congenial ground for reformers, abolitionists, temperance advocates, and feminists. Having grown up outside established churches, spiritualists were naturally suspicious of all hierarchies, ecclesiastical or civil.

Women played a particularly important role in the spread of spiritualism because anyone at all, even women, could be the source of divine truth, as messages from the spirit world were claimed to be. Mediums needed no special training at seminaries or universities, which excluded women. Nor did mediums need to be sanctified by church authorities, who excluded women from the pulpit. In fact, if one sex seemed to be more appropriately constituted to be mediums, it was the female, whose body brought forth life.

Spiritualism also provided women with a means of claiming authority, and Victoria Woodhull learned early how to profit from this. Profound social taboos inhibited most women from speaking in public. To call attention to oneself in a public square was considered not only unlady-like, but a form of treachery to a husband, whom a woman would shame by straying so far from her proper place at his hearth. But as an instrument of God's will, a medium was excused from such rebuke. She was not, after all, speaking in her own voice. Throughout her career, Victoria Woodhull claimed that all her important decisions were dictated by spirit voices, all of her most spectacular utterances made in trances.

Speaking in trances as a clairvoyant and as a medical healer, Victoria Woodhull reaped what she later called a golden harvest. She believed that her gifts as a medical healer saved her baby Byron from a severe illness. Unfortunately, she could not heal the damage that prevented his mental growth. Though no longer a baby, the child could not talk, nor dress or clean himself. His terrible helplessness was a continual reproach to Woodhull, who prayed to God for another child, a child healthy in body and mind.

In the spring of 1861, while North and South were preparing for civil war, Zulu Maud Woodhull was born. No icicles clung to her bedframe as they had when Byron was born, but Canning staggered out of the house after the delivery, leaving his wife and new child in distress. Victoria pounded for help on the walls of her room with a broken chair rung that she seized from the floor. Finally a neighbor heard the noise and came to help, climbing up from the basement where she had removed a grating to get into the house. Little Zulu Maud was pronounced healthy, but Victoria Woodhull's willingness to endure Canning was ebbing. She related to Theodore Tilton that a few days later, sitting propped up on her bed, she looked out the

Colonel James Harvey Blood sought Victoria Woodhull's help as a spiritualist and medium when he was troubled by nightmares about fallen Civil War comrades. After the dissolution of their marriage, he regretted that "the grandest woman in the world went back on me."

window and caught sight of her husband, "staggering up the steps of a house across the way, mistaking it for his own." "Why should I any longer live with this man?" she asked herself.

Divorces were becoming more common in the United States, but they were still not easy to obtain, particularly if it was the wife who wished to divorce her husband. Simply wanting a divorce was not enough reason to be granted one, even if the request were made by both husband and wife. Nor would a husband's drunkenness alone secure his unfortunate wife a divorce. In 1831 a judge had written that "Courts of justice do not pretend to furnish cures for all the miseries of human life." In fact, reasoned the courts, a man wrecking his life with drink was all the more in need of a helpful caring wife, a woman whose duty lay in accepting him and, she might hope, reforming him.

Still, judges did want to distinguish between virtuous husbands and vicious husbands. Victoria Woodhull obtained a divorce from Canning in Chicago in 1865. Certainly he had abandoned her, and his indifference to the welfare of his newborn daughter would have shocked the sensibilities of midcentury America, where motherhood and family were becoming sacred.

Woodhull finally sought her divorce from Canning because, at 27 years of age, she had met someone else with whom she wished to share her life. Colonel James Harvey Blood, a wounded veteran, was recently returned from the Civil War, where he had served valiantly as a regimental commander. Trailing memories of wounded and dying soldiers, Colonel Blood was comforted by his sense that his companions lived on as spirits. When he came to Victoria Woodhull for advice, she found a tall and handsome war hero who bore himself with a quiet dignity that matched her own. His destiny, she told him, was to become her husband. She delivered her message, she told her biographer Tilton, in a trancelike state.

Like other spiritualists, Blood and Woodhull believed that true marriages were unions of spiritual affinities, essences that sought each other. Woodhull did not accept that Blood's marriage to another was an impediment. She believed his marriage to be "morally sundered," she told Tilton later, as was her own. She was ready to abandon the belief that laws made unions sacred. Nothing holy attached her to the drunken Canning Woodhull. Resolved to make his life with her, Blood rented a bell-fringed surrey, and became her business manager and advance man as Woodhull told fortunes and practiced healing from village to village in the Midwest. When they had enough money, they paid off Blood's debts, obtained their divorces, and were married. He was a fortunate choice, respected by those who knew him. The publisher Benjamin Tucker late in his life reconsidered his youthful admiration for Victoria Woodhull, but not for Colonel Blood, whom he called "an honest, whole-souled, open-hearted, generous gentleman."

Colonel Blood continued the informal education of Victoria Woodhull. This reflective, philosophical man had long been an advocate of reforms. At a time when men of property could pay to avoid military duty, he had fought in the Civil War because of his conviction that slavery was evil. Now believing in women's rights and labor reform, Blood taught Woodhull that the conditions that had created her poverty and her unhappy marriage could be altered.

With a sober and hardworking man at her side, Woodhull felt ready to rescue her sister Tennie from the unwholesome company of the Claflins. Tennie, distraught, was supporting a dozen to twenty Claflin relatives with her dubious healing. Woodhull recalled Tennie's despair for Tilton. "My God," Tennie wept to her sister, "have I got to live this life always?" Moved at last to resist the Claflins, Woodhull "clutched Tennie as by main force and flung her out of this semi-humbug." Buck and Annie were outraged at Tennie's departure, blaming Colonel Blood for encouraging not one but two appealing and talented daughters to leave the family business and set forth on their own.

Meanwhile, Woodhull was planning a new move. Clairvoyance and healing were becoming endangered professions. The established churches questioned the honesty of mediums, and the medical profession was driving unlicensed practitioners out of the field. "Delusion and quackery," huffed the *New York Herald* about spiritualism. As always, when she felt compelled to explain a decision, Woodhull enlisted the agency of a helpful spirit. As she sat at a marble table in a Pittsburgh rooming house one evening, she later told Tilton, a spirit guide suddenly illumined the room by writing a simple command in English letters upon the table. She must go to New York City and begin her great work of reform. The spirit guide revealed himself as Demosthenes, the ancient Greek orator. If Victoria Woodhull was to be one of those good people whose works improve the world, she must, like Demosthenes, use her greatest gift—her voice.

Just as she had left San Francisco in obedience to a voice she had heard, so too she would go to New York, a city where millionaires were made every day in another form of gold rush. This golden harvest lay not along meandering stream beds, but instead on the stock exchanges, where men passed papers among each other and some of them grew extremely rich.

The "Lady Brokers," Victoria Woodhull and Tennessee Claflin, crack their whips over the Wall Street "bears" and "bulls"—symbols for the traders whose commands to buy or sell drive the stock market up or down. Both the top bull and bear are shipping tycoon Cornelius Vanderbilt, who, according to gossip, had proposed marriage to Tennessee but was refused.

GOTHAM: BROKER, CANDIDATE, AND JOURNALIST

We went into Wall street, not particularly because I wanted to be a broker in stocks and gold, but because I wanted to plant the flag of woman's rebellion in the very centre of the continent.
—Victoria Woodhull in *Woodhull and Claflin's Weekly,* October 18, 1873

When Victoria Woodhull arrived in New York in 1868, the city was still lit by gas lamps. The streets were muddy, and barnyard animals roamed among the wooden huts in the ramshackle neighborhood just south of Central Park. The new telegraph and telephone wires, hastily hung, lay like great cobwebs across old timber poles. Horses pulled the streetcars, and garbage flung from tenement windows fouled walkways. Only the rich could pay the fees to clean the streets. The poor lived with manure and refuse underfoot, no respite from the dank, dark hovels they called home.

Trailing at their daughters' heels, the Claflins followed Colonel Blood, Victoria Woodhull, and her sister Tennessee to New York. Lured by the money the sisters might earn, Buck and Annie, along with two other married daughters and their husbands and eight children, took rooms in lower Manhattan, while Woodhull looked around her for the destiny her spirit guide had promised. Whatever such destiny might be, the Claflins would settle like prairie dust into any home she made.

The Woodhulls and Claflins passed easily into the tumult of urban life. Although the city was proud of its colonial past and the old Dutch families who prospered there, New York sported a rough-and-tumble quality in the years after the Civil War. Like a boomtown, the city was changing fast. In 1868, almost a million people lived in Manhattan, most of them crowded onto the southern tip of that island. Some of the newcomers had come from Europe in the wake of the unsuccessful revolutions of midcentury, bringing with them ideas about social and economic justice.

Indeed, workers were not prospering, although American industry was growing rapidly. Despite the promise of more money from the spread of the railroads and from new industries in post–Civil War America, wages and working conditions for many were worse than they had

Often satirized in cartoons by Thomas Nast, Democratic party head William "Boss" Tweed was convicted of robbing New York City of millions of dollars. He died in 1878 in the Ludlow Street Jail, where Victoria Woodhull was a fellow inmate.

been when most men and women worked on farms or in small shops. When the railroads hit bad times, industrial tycoons cut workers' wages and kept enormous salaries for themselves and their stockholders. Meanwhile, economic adventurers made quick profits on the unregulated stock exchange. With bogus enterprises masquerading as legitimate businesses, corrupt financiers profited. No city was more dishonestly managed than New York, whose mayor, Boss Tweed, kept his thoroughbred horses in mahogany stables. "What are you going to do about it?" was his retort to his critics.

Victoria Woodhull was no stranger to the hard lot of working people when she came to New York. The house at 17 Great Jones Street, where she installed her family, was on the part of East Third Street that lay between the posh bordellos of Broadway and the teeming street life of Bowery pickpockets, pimps, and prostitutes. The department stores and theaters of New York thrived alongside the carpentry shops, lumberyards, and houses of prostitution. The city was rapidly becoming the vice capital of the country. "As everyone knows," observed a New York police chief, "the city is being rebuilt and vice moves ahead of business."

Victoria Woodhull had found her way before into crowded streets where theaters, businesses, and brothels flourished. Her apprenticeship in San Francisco during the tumultuous years of the Gold Rush had served up useful lessons. She knew that idle talk about buying and selling passed easily from tycoons to mistresses in the elegant bordellos of lower Manhattan. Such chatter lined the pockets of savvy brothel owners whose "girls" were trained to listen carefully to the business plans of important clients. One elegant woman of fashion, privy to insider financial secrets, was Woodhull's old actress friend from San Francisco, Josie Mansfield, whom financier Jim Fisk kept in emeralds and ball gowns. Whatever tremors might shake the New York Stock Exchange, Josie Mansfield was well placed to predict them to her friend Victoria Woodhull.

Also near Great Jones Street was the office of one of those millionaires whose climb to riches was the stuff of legend. Cornelius Vanderbilt, the steamship and railroad tycoon, was now a curmudgeonly 73-year-old, quarrelsome and tyrannical. Guiltily, he mourned the death of a wife he had both abused and betrayed. Nor had he much comfort from the uneven careers of his sons, whom he had also bullied. More recently, some investments had even gone bad. Vanderbilt was alone and lonely, someone who neither wholly believed in spirits nor entirely discounted them.

After they had settled in, Woodhull and Tennessee called on Vanderbilt. They offered their services as clairvoyants who could make stock-market predictions, or, if Vanderbilt preferred his own hunches, as medical healers who could restore the spirits of lonely old men. Vanderbilt was smitten with Tennie, whom he called his "little sparrow." Though he generally gave advice seekers short shrift, Vanderbilt admired these two attractive and spunky women, perhaps sensing in them the same restless energy that had taken him from farming on Staten Island to the pinnacles of financial power. Although Vanderbilt would not make their fortune for them, he was willing to help.

Woodhull had not come East, however, only to seek out men like Vanderbilt, no matter how useful such an acquaintance would be. Colonel Blood had taught her that reformers could engage themselves in a field of struggle as vital as a revival preacher's battle for souls. In New York, Woodhull joined a vast and important marketplace where ideas for political reform were hawked, weighed, and measured as vigorously as if they were commodities on the stock exchange. But before she became a player in these debates, Woodhull schooled herself in the arguments.

In January 1869, some months after meeting Vanderbilt, she began her informal education. She traveled to Washington, D.C., to attend the first national convention of the woman suffrage movement. In Caroll Hall, where a hardworking furnace belched smoke against the winter cold, Woodhull heard the great figures of the women's movement for the first time. Here were the movement's strategist Susan B. Anthony and its philosopher Elizabeth Cady Stanton, women who had carried the torch for women's political and economic freedoms for twenty years. Here, too, was Frederick Douglass, who had escaped from slavery in his youth and joined the struggle for its abolition. Douglass's oratory had awakened the slumbering conscience of the nation in the years before the Civil War.

The abolitionists and woman suffrage leaders, who had worked together in the 1840s and 1850s, were now parting company. Just half a year earlier, in July 1868, the 14th Amendment to the Constitution had been ratified, guaranteeing citizenship to all persons born in the United States and to all naturalized citizens. Even as the women's convention assembled, Congress debated the passage of the 15th Amendment, an amendment that would secure voting rights for black men, but not for women, black or white. The question facing the Washington convention was whether or not to demand suffrage for women along with black men. On their part, Anthony and Stanton were urging the United States Congress to pass a 16th Amendment that would extend suffrage to women. They felt betrayed by the abolitionists, who had sought and received their help, promising to turn to woman suffrage as soon as the war ended. Now the abolitionists were delaying the call for woman suffrage.

It was the "Negro's hour," argued Frederick Douglass. As he transcribed his speech later, Douglass recalled saying, "Woman has a thousand ways to attach herself to the governing power of the land . . . it cannot be pretended her cause is as urgent as ours." But Anthony and Stanton denied that intimacy with a powerful man could ever ensure a woman's well-being. Earlier, Anthony had persuaded the New York State legislature to pass a bill securing a wife's rights to her own property, replacing laws in that state that treated a married woman like a child. Only two years later, as the women's movement shifted its focus to support the Civil War, the legislature reversed most of those reforms. If women did not have the political clout of the vote, Anthony and Stanton believed, the extension of civil rights to them would proceed with glacial slowness.

Stanton was herself a classical scholar, brilliantly eloquent in several languages, the educated daughter of a doting lawyer father, although a father who had looked askance at her career in public life. Stanton was weary of being continually degraded as unworthy of the vote because she was—according to the popular science of her time—by nature mentally inferior to any man.

As they planned the platform and strategy of their difficult and broadly unpopular campaign, both Stanton and Anthony made decisions that would return to plague them. Saying that she would take money even from the devil himself in the cause of woman suffrage, Anthony had accepted help from George Francis Train, an eccentric labor reformer whose racist opinions quite understandably horrified the abolitionists. Stanton herself asked if black men should indeed vote before white women, saying that "Sambo," the derogatory term of her time, who could not read the Declaration of Independence should not make laws for educated women.

Positioned against the New York wing headed by Anthony and Stanton was the Boston wing of the woman

Women's rights campaigners, Susan B. Anthony (left) and Elizabeth Cady Stanton had great respect for Victoria Woodhull. They admired her status as independently wealthy since most women's rights supporters depended solely on their husbands.

suffrage movement. This wing included Lucy Stone, the New Englander who had fought for the right to retain her own name after marriage, her husband, the abolitionist Henry Blackwell, and Henry Ward Beecher, the popular Brooklyn minister who became president of their association. The Boston wing reflected the more conservative and conventional sentiments of New England. Many of the more conservative suffragists were not pleased with Stanton and Anthony's newspaper *The Revolution,* whose title alone made them uneasy. They were resolutely unsympathetic to the union movement and workers' strikes, which Anthony supported. Moreover, in their journal Stanton and Anthony had expressed tolerant opinions on the subject of divorce and had aired discussions of birth control. New York State only permitted divorce if adultery could be proved. For two decades Elizabeth Cady Stanton had been urging that divorce laws be reformed. Lucy Stone agreed with Stanton that a loveless marriage was immoral, but, fearful of controversy and wishing to protect the ideal of family life, she had urged Stanton not to bring these "social" issues, as they were called, into the women's rights debate.

Woodhull was drawn to the more radical wing of the convention, as were many midwestern and western women. When Elizabeth Cady Stanton rose to speak, she urged women to inspire men to work for better purposes. Sitting in the audience, Woodhull was stirred with the presentiment of a mission. "I thought the millennium was at hand," she later told a reporter from the *New York Herald*. She, who had sat through so many revival meetings in prairie campgrounds, recognized a passionate trumpet call to arms. She believed in women "most completely," she told a journalist from the *New York World* who was covering the convention. And yet, she added, she "also believed in man just as thoroughly." Impressed, the journalist wrote up his story about the interesting "Mrs. Woodhull," whom he called "the coming woman."

Though moved, Woodhull hesitated to endorse Stanton's exclusive appeal to one half of humanity alone to reform all injustice. Indeed, although she was sympathetic to the New York wing of the movement, she did not see herself reflected completely in their company. None of these women was anything like herself, trailing a crew of noisy Claflins. Many of the suffragist leaders were proud of their family connections, having been raised in comfort and refinement and given the finest educations the times permitted women, in genteel seminaries or from a father's well-stocked library. They were all too willing to trade on their social prestige to advance the reforms they believed in.

Too often, like Elizabeth Cady Stanton at the convention, they betrayed the prejudices of their origins, offering patronizing or denigrating remarks about less educated working men and women, black or white.

To someone like Victoria Woodhull, who had come up the hard way, the cultivated manners and genteel aversions of the delegates around her were insulting and irrelevant. The working women she had known had no time for such deportment—actresses in San Francisco; healers and mediums in Ohio, Indiana and Illinois; the streetwalkers of lower Broadway and the Bowery, whose worn young faces she passed daily in the neighborhood of Great Jones Street. "Teacup hurricanes," she wrote somewhat dismissively of the convention, when she recalled these meetings years later in private notes. Still, Woodhull left Washington inspired with a sense of mission, and she had also learned some valuable lessons. She had glimpsed how the argument for woman suffrage might be made as she listened to Virginia Minor from Missouri declare that because women were citizens the Constitution already guaranteed their right to vote. Here lay an argument that might make a new amendment for woman suffrage unnecessary.

She had also learned that the women's movement needed money, and that positions of influence would probably fall to women who could supply this lack. Victoria Woodhull was nobody important's daughter or wife, but she knew about making money. During her short residence in New York, she had become well acquainted with those back-room parlors where brokers, bankers, and financiers passed around information along with whiskey and cigars. She returned to New York, where Commodore Cornelius Vanderbilt and the operations of the New York Stock Exchange lay waiting to serve her.

Months later, Woodhull took advantage of frenzied speculation on the gold market and made a small fortune on Wall Street. A few investors, one of them Josie Mansfield's lover Jim Fisk, had attempted to corner the gold market. The value of the precious metal had been unstable since a cheaper currency called "greenbacks," not backed by gold reserves, had been issued to finance the Civil War. On September 15, 1869, acting on false information that suggested the price of gold would rise, unwary speculators crowded the sidewalks outside the stock exchange in a fever of buying. Later in the day when the earlier rumors were proved false, the frenzy to sell was equally loud. In the midst of the mayhem, Woodhull was unperturbed and confident, occupying a carriage outside the exchange from which she issued careful instructions to representatives on the floor.

No one can be completely sure how Victoria Woodhull knew when to buy and sell. She may have been acting on reliable information passed on to her by her friend Josie Mansfield. And she may have passed on such useful tips, disguised as clairvoyant visions, to the great tycoon Commodore Vanderbilt himself, a man who would know how to show his gratitude. Like so many other players in the financial markets, Woodhull kept her secrets.

By the end of "Black Friday," as the fateful day was called, many stockbrokers in New York and across the country were ruined, and innumerable personal fortunes had been lost. "I came out a winner," reported Woodhull later to the *Herald,* recounting her good luck. She claimed she had invested as much as $100,000, the whole of her earnings as a clairvoyant, in the speculation. Woodhull remained vague about the precise size of her personal fortune, before and after Black Friday. She may have found some advantage in exaggerating her holdings whenever such an inflation might be useful. But certainly Woodhull was now a woman of considerable means, with, she told the *Herald,* perhaps more than a half million dollars to broker—a fortune worth ten times as much by today's standards. Nor had opportunities for investment ended after Black Friday. With stocks tumbling after the gold panic, bargains for shrewd investors like Woodhull offered new chances for enrichment.

Moreover, she had learned that a new community of women with money to invest was interested in the stock exchange. Teachers, housewives who had saved up the allowances doled out to them by their husbands, writers, proprietors of small businesses, heiresses with fortunes, and madams of brothels all had money in their pockets. A woman like herself who had steered her investment through the treacherous shoals of Black Friday might reasonably turn to investing for others. She lacked only a seat on the New York Stock Exchange, one that would permit her to buy and sell securities on the floor of the exchange on her own behalf or as an agent for others.

These places were in fact real, numbered seats—comfortable-enough chairs where designated members sat for the twice-daily auctions of stock, before the institution of continuous selling with agents rushing to and fro. Fortunately for Victoria Woodhull, in 1869 it was possible to buy a seat on the stock exchange from another member. Only a few years earlier, new members could join the exchange only if an older one died or resigned, and only after the membership had voted the new member one of themselves, past the dreaded "blackball" by which a few voters could exclude anyone. Because of the entrenched prejudice against women working in such a public marketplace as finance, it is unlikely Woodhull would have glided through such an election.

Buoyed by the change in the rules of stock-exchange membership, Woodhull called upon Commodore Vanderbilt and told him that her spirit advisors wanted her to open a brokerage. Vanderbilt called her a "bold operator," as indeed he had reason to believe, having watched her at work. Vanderbilt handed her a check for $7,000, more than enough money to buy a seat on the exchange. More importantly, by handing Woodhull the check he lent her his name. Any bank where such a check might be proffered would know that the great tycoon Cornelius Vanderbilt himself was backing Victoria Woodhull and her sister Tennessee. All of New York's financial world would learn soon after.

In January of the New Year 1870, the sisters sent a brief notice to the *New York Herald* advertising that their firm, Woodhull, Claflin and Co., was open for business. The opening of a new brokerage house was not usually considered newsworthy, but when the proprietors of the brokerage had women's names, enterprising journalists took note. The *Herald* sent a reporter to the parlor rooms at the Hoffmann House, a new hotel on 24th Street, where the sisters had rented two rooms for their fledgling firm. The *Herald* ran a gently mocking article about the young brokers under the headline "Queens of Finance."

After they read the *Herald*'s piece, Woodhull and Tennie invited the reporter to call again. Admitted to the parlor rooms, now empty of the first-day crowds, the reporter found furnishings designed to impress. Paintings hung on the wall, statuary decorated the corners, a piano stood among the ample upholstered sofas and chairs. One small frame contained the motto "Simply to thy Cross I cling." Nearby hung a picture of Commodore Vanderbilt. Woodhull and her sister were telling the world that they were prosperous and well-connected, but also pious and feminine. They meant to inspire confidence and frighten no one.

Tennie greeted the reporter. Surely she found it "awkward" as a woman to be a broker, suggested the reporter. Tennie was amused. "If I noticed what society said," she responded "I could never leave my apartments except in fantastic walking dress or in ballroom costume; but I despise what

THE QUEENS OF FINANCE.

A New Phase of the Woman's Rights Question.

The Lady Stock Operators of Wall Street— The Firm of Woodhull, Claflin & Co.— Vanderbilt's Protégés—Interview of a Herald Reporter with the Future Princesses of Erie.

Early in Woodhull's career, the New York Herald *hailed her as a "queen of finance." It gave her generous column space, where she stated her platform as a Presidential candidate.*

squeamy, crying girls or powdered counter-jumping dandies say of me." When Woodhull entered, dressed plainly and with no ornament other than the single rose in her hair, the reporter noticed that she was older than Tennie and perhaps more sensitively wrought. Woodhull, unlike her sister, kept her interview to business matters. She stated that she had won a fortune on Black Friday and meant to invest money in railroads and mining. The reporter wrote a description of the interview, which ran this time under the more respectful head "The Queens of Finance: A New Phase of the Woman's Rights Question." The *Herald* proclaimed pompously their continual interest in those "various isolated instances in which women have stepped aside and engaged in pursuits and reaped profits from which from time immemorial have been considered as the sole vested rights of the other sex."

Some weeks after the reporter from the *Herald* filed his story, another determined journalist crossed town to interview the brokers, who were now housed at 44 Broad Street—larger quarters near the stock exchange—having had a prosperous first month. Susan B. Anthony had read the derisive reports of the opening of Woodhull and Claflin. She was well acquainted with the sneers and laughter that accompanied any woman's breaching of the conventional barriers that separated men's work from women's. She rejoiced that another stronghold had fallen, and wrote of the victory in her newspaper, *The Revolution*. As Susan B. Anthony left the brokerage, she passed a waiter bringing hot luncheon food up to the sisters. Soon, Anthony reflected, women would be able to use the vote to put food into their mouths without needing to ask men for permission. Meanwhile, here were Woodhull and Claflin earning hundreds of dollars a week, rather than, as Tennie had observed with mild audacity, sewing underpants for ten cents a pair.

Still fairly new to New York City, Woodhull and her sister were ebullient, confident, and daring. With Colonel Blood as the experienced accountant and silent partner of the brokerage, and with Vanderbilt a daily visitor and powerful counselor, the firm of Woodhull, Claflin and Co. was securely launched. When Tennie one day foiled a would-be swindler attempting to pass a forged check, the *Herald* cheered that "the ladies" had met their first challenge and passed "with flying colors."

To be sure, no one knew quite how seriously to value the professional skills of the new brokers. Most of the men who worked on Wall Street found it improbable that a woman had a talent for making a fortune on the stock exchange. These men assumed that all important decisions for the Woodhull and Claflin brokerage were made by Commodore Vanderbilt. They also assumed, more accurately, that Colonel Blood was responsible for the management and accounting. But the contract the sisters drew up with Colonel Blood ensured that no major financial decision could be made without their approval.

It was a mistake to underrate Woodhull's business acumen or mock the nerve center she operated in the back rooms of the brokerage, where information about buying and selling on the exchange came freely from knowledgeable sources. Woodhull had been a sharp trader on rough roads all over the Midwest, and she knew the value of insider information and how to obtain it.

Out in the front rooms on Broad Street, Colonel Blood labored over the accounts. Wily old Buck Claflin, kept at a safe distance from the actual business, was installed behind an ornate desk and passed off to reporters as a beloved parent who had taught law to his young daughters before misfortune and loss impoverished him. Behind a richly carved walnut partition inset with decorated glass, the sisters dispensed champagne and chocolate-covered strawberries in their private offices to the women who sought them out by a separate entrance. One madam of a Manhattan house of prostitution claimed that Woodhull and Claflin returned her a profit of $30,000 in one year. Such investors passed on business gossip that was as valuable to the brokerage business as the profits they made.

Nor were the sisters averse to advertising themselves, playing for publicity in newspapers in a way that more contemporary entrepreneurs might admire. They understood that curiosity about themselves as "female brokers" could be transformed into profitable patronage, and they unabashedly marketed flamboyant images of themselves. They often wore men's suits, willing to provoke scandal by flouting dress customs in return for newspaper attention. On another day the sisters might wear matching purple velvet gowns or sport solid-gold pens tucked behind their ears, all their curls newly cropped in a boyish style. The *Herald* called them "the sensation of New York," and the "bewitching brokers." Tennie was flirtatious, uninhibited, and strikingly pretty. Her older sister Victoria was more reserved, beautiful when animated in speech, and seemed to talk to men with a confident authority not typical of women. So many men came to the offices of Woodhull and Claflin that the sisters printed a sign telling them to "state their business and retire."

Although the New York press applauded the new brokerage firm of Victoria Woodhull and Tennessee Claflin, they did not take the "Bewitching Brokers" too seriously. The sisters were often portrayed as "inspiring many flashy young men to visit [the new] establishment . . . and showing off their exquisite figures."

Another small triumph lay waiting. After the close of the business day, it was the custom on Wall Street for bankers and brokers to pass a pleasant supper hour at Delmonico's restaurant, where by longstanding tradition ladies were not welcomed unless they were accompanied by a man. One evening, Woodhull and Tennie passed through the doors of the restaurant and made their way to be seated. Embarrassed, the host told them he could not seat them. The resourceful Tennie stepped outside, collared an idle carriage driver and sat him down with her sister. "Tomato soup for three," she told the waiter, who shuffled off to the kitchen to bring them their dinner. Wall Street and Delmonico's restaurant had been breached, but other arenas of masculine privilege would prove less easy to assault.

Now a wealthy businesswoman, Woodhull meant to look the part. Anyone strolling near Fifth Avenue in the Murray Hill neighborhood of Manhattan that early winter of 1870 might have seen workmen carrying rolls of Oriental carpeting into one of the brownstone mansions on 38th Street. Inside the mansion, Venetian glass chandeliers were being hung from mirrored and frescoed ceilings. Bolts of damask and gold-fringed silk were carried into the boudoirs on the upper floors. Behind the columned windows that looked out onto the sidewalk on the first floor, heavy velvet curtains were transforming the parlor rooms. The young owner was the Wall Street broker Victoria Woodhull, who was moving her family uptown into the newly fashionable midtown neighborhood. She was entering public life, and she meant to do so on a grand scale.

All of the Woodhulls and Claflins moved into the brownstone mansion in Murray Hill. At last Buck and Annie Claflin were living in the comfort they had dreamed of while they tended their grist mill on the Ohio prairie. But most likely the decor of the mansion exceeded even their flights of fancy. With incense burners hanging from the ceilings and birds singing in a greenhouse off the parlor, the house made visitors feel that they had been transported magically to an Oriental palace. Woodhull knew the value of advertising the power of money, and now that she had some she would not be shy about using either the currency or its influence.

She also bore no illusions about her limited schooling. Woodhull and her sister were street smart. From old Buck Claflin, they had learned to smell a bad check when it crossed their counter, and they could calculate the risk of an investment. But Colonel Blood was not only left to do the bookkeeping at the brokerage, he acted as secretary as well. Before the invention of typewriters or word processors, the hallmarks of good schooling and middle-class manners were elaborate styles of penmanship. Acquaintances familiar with Colonel Blood's elegant script recognized his hand in Victoria Woodhull's formal correspondence. She would have betrayed the simple schooling of her frontier childhood with the loose, unpunctuated writing she used in private letters to her family.

At the same time, Woodhull understood her strengths. She had learned in San Francisco that hers was a compelling presence on stage, one that bound an audience to her voice. The religious mysticism that had shaped her childhood left her unsatisfied with earning and spending money as the final outcome of a life nobly lived. She believed in human progress, as had the makers of the American Revolution more than a hundred years earlier. As the nineteenth century moved through its second half, she shared with her countrymen an expectation that the dawn of the new century would surely be accompanied by an elevation in the human spirit. Since the Washington women's convention, when Stanton's words had breathed fire into her soul, she had been convinced that both law and custom hampered the progress of men and women. But her political education, begun by Colonel Blood, was informal and unfocused. The parlor rooms at the Murray Hill mansion, opened to artists, politicians, and intellectuals, became a salon for heady talk about reform. Woodhull was developing a political position from which to analyze industrial capitalism, the economic exchange system in which she had so lately prospered.

Rocked by the cycles of boom and bust that could leave the weakest members of society without livelihood, industrial capitalism seemed a harsh system that replaced the more beneficent relationship of master and apprentice with an indifference to workers' welfare, if not downright cruelty. The factories and the new railroad and mining industries attracted laborers who became entrenched in the growing cities as a fixed working class, a class unlike any the nation had known before. Since the pool of available laborers was far greater than what the infant factory systems needed, owners could easily dictate the conditions of employment without fear of losing their workforce. To make matters worse, the new urban dwellers were isolated from traditional networks of family, and felt displaced as well as stuck in poverty.

Like the Claflins, who had moved out to Ohio and then vagabonded around Iowa, Indiana, and Illinois before going east again, vast numbers of Americans migrated from place to place. They might settle on the westward frontier or take up residence in the new cities that grew up with the development of the Erie Canal and Great Lakes shipping routes: Syracuse, Rochester, Buffalo, Detroit, or Chicago. Such dislocation bred new dissatisfactions. With old patterns of work altered and long-time associations with familiar places severed, some Americans were willing to question the values that underlay unregulated industrial capitalism, such as its ruthless competition and its assumption of rugged, self-interested individualism.

The national mood before the Civil War was fertile ground for new ideas, particularly the new visions of community life that were based on cooperation rather than competition, or on friendship and love rather than isolation. Some of these early alternative visions were religious, rising from convictions that godly truths had been revealed to fortunate prophets. In 1847, followers of the prophet Joseph Smith, founder of the Mormon Church, crossed the Rocky Mountains and settled in Salt Lake City to shape a community according to their interpretation of divine law. Other founders of experimental communities were secular; some of these based their notions of community life on the ideas of European socialists. For example, Robert Owen, a Scottish industrialist, created a community of his own workers and then migrated to the United States, where in 1825 he established a socialist settlement in Indiana called New Harmony. But whether religious or secular, these visionaries dreamed of utopias, or perfect societies. They took the name "utopia" (a word meaning "no place") from the title of Sir Thomas More's 16th-century essay describing an imaginary ideal community.

One of these utopian visionaries was a tall, hawk-nosed New Englander named Stephen Pearl Andrews, who found his way to Victoria Woodhull's parlor in the mansion in Murray Hill. When he met Woodhull, Andrews was 61 years old, a man who had already established and disbanded two hopeful utopias of his own design. Short on money, Andrews was still rich in convictions and the courage to state them. As a young man he had been run out of Texas for preaching abolition, barely escaping with his life. Later he established an experimental community on Long Island called "Modern Times," where members traded in a currency called "labor hours" and extracted no profits above what a product cost in time to create. Like many utopian reformers, Andrews believed above all that the rights of an individual were greater than the rights of government. Because they were sovereign in their own domain, individuals should brook no interference from the state, which was constituted only to defend their freedoms.

No realm of individual freedom should be more inviolate, according to Andrews and other reformers, than the private realm of sexual life. In their visions of improved societies, reformers boldly reshaped family life and the intimate relations between husband and wife. The religious community of the Shakers, for example, required sexual abstinence. Until 1890, the Mormon Church officially encouraged what it called "plural marriage" or polygamy, which permitted a man to have more than one wife. These religious critics of traditional marriage claimed divine law as their inspiration. Secular critics of the family drew justification from the crassly economic basis of marriage. They condemned marriage as an alliance intended only to secure the protection of inherited property by claiming some children as "legitimate," rather than an alliance to enable the happiness of two people. With its cumbersome divorce laws and its insistence on monogamy, the civil contract of marriage was the antithesis of freedom, affirmed Andrews.

Woodhull acquired from Andrews a vision of a community with human beings bound to each other by their shared understanding of a good higher than profit. With such a vision of an economic, political, and social utopia, Woodhull sought entry onto a national stage where she could mount her argument. She was already good news copy, dear to the staff writers in the *Herald*'s news room as one of the two "lady brokers." She meant to continue to provide good copy. As for Stephen Pearl Andrews, he recognized in Victoria Woodhull someone who had the means and ambition to bring his ideas before the public, although he may not have anticipated how spectacularly she meant to do so.

On April 2, 1870, Woodhull announced her candidacy for the Presidency of the United States, in the election to be held two years later. Although she was unable to vote for herself, there was no constitutional barrier requiring that the Presidency be occupied only by a man. In a letter to the *Herald,* Woodhull separated herself from the "teacup hurricanes" of the middle-class woman suffrage movement, citing with pride her own self-made achievements. "While others of my sex devoted themselves to a crusade against the laws that shackle the women of the country," she said, "I asserted my individual independence; while others prayed for the good time coming, I worked for it; while others argued for the equality of woman with man, I proved it by successfully engaging in business, while others sought to show that there was no valid reason why woman should be treated socially and politically as a being inferior to man, I boldly entered the arena of politics and business and exercised the rights I already possessed. I therefore claim the right to speak for the unenfranchised women of the country. . . ."

Although Woodhull spoke confidently of her Presidential ambitions, she was not so unrealistic as to imagine she could mount a competitive candidacy. Woodhull later wrote in her journal *The Humanitarian* that she used her campaign to draw public attention to women's claims of equality with men, and indeed her purpose seems to have been to find an audience for her platforms. But the platform she represented would be far broader than a campaign for women's rights alone. Like Anthony and Stanton before her, who had championed the labor movement in the pages of the *Revolution,* Woodhull's engagement in women's rights led her to embrace a more general campaign of reform as well.

The utopian planner Stephen Pearl Andrews was responsible for the precision with which her candidacy spelled out its calls for prison reform, for relief for the poor, and for an improved management of foreign policy. The *Herald* greeted Woodhull's candidacy with a familiar mix of admiration and amusement, but noted shrewdly that the "lady broker of Broad Street" was "independent of all suffrage tea parties." Nor was she a "Mrs. Grundy," they added, using the derisive term for middle class women engaged in moral reform. The *Herald* generously provided Woodhull with column space where long letters on the nature of government were pub-

THE RISING TIDE OF REFORM

Victoria Woodhull declared herself a candidate for the Presidency of the United States in the election of 1872. She explained her candidacy in a letter to the New York Herald *on April 2, 1870, calling herself a "representative woman" who, having achieved equality with men in business, would campaign for woman suffrage.*

I am well aware that in assuming this position I shall evoke more ridicule than enthusiasm at the outset. But this is an epoch of sudden changes and startling surprises. What may appear absurd to-day will assume a serious aspect to-morrow. I am content to wait until my claim for recognition as a candidate shall receive the calm consideration of the press and the public. The blacks were cattle in 1860; a negro now sits in Jeff Davis' seat in the United States Senate. The sentiment of the country was, even in 1863, against negro suffrage; now the negro's right to vote is acknowledged by the Constitution of the United States. Let those, therefore, who ridiculed the negro's claim to exercise the right to "life, liberty and the pursuit of happiness," and who lived to see him vote and hold high public office, ridicule the aspirations of the women of the country for complete political equality as much as they please. They cannot roll back the rising tide of reform. The world moves. . . . All that has been said and written hitherto in support of equality for woman has had its proper effect on the public mind. . . . My candidature for the Presidency will, I confidently expect, develop the fact that the principles of equal rights for all have taken deep root.

I anticipate criticism; but however unfavourable the comment this letter may evoke I trust that my sincerity will not be called in question. I have deliberately and of my own accord placed myself before the people as a candidate for the Presidency of the United States, and having the means, courage, energy and strength necessary for the race, intend to contest it to the close.

lished under her name. Most people familiar with Stephen Pearl Andrews' work recognized the sentiments and style, the long rehearsing of ancient history and the call for a new universal world government as his voice.

It was as natural for Victoria Woodhull to use the words of Stephen Pearl Andrews as it was for her to claim that the spirit world dictated her speeches. Raised in the tradition of religious revival, she believed that it mattered little which person voiced a truth, so long as the truth was voiced. With a platform to argue and a candidacy to draw fire, Victoria Woodhull freed herself from requiring the *Herald* or any of the other New York newspapers to provide her with access to an audience. She founded her own journal for a nation of avid consumers of newsprint.

On May 21, 1870, Woodhull published the first edition of *Woodhull and Claflin's Weekly,* which provided a forum for women suffragists, political reformers, and writers, as well as a sounding board for her unprecedented Presidential candidacy. Only a day earlier, the *Revolution,* proudly and lovingly published by Anthony and Stanton, passed on to new owners. The *Revolution* had been controversial and wide-ranging in its interests, arguing for currency, land, and labor reforms and advocating the formation of a labor-based reform party. But without the support of the prosperous women of the conservative Boston wing of the woman suffrage movement, the *Revolution* foundered, heavily in debt. The *Weekly* would take up the cause of radical reforms in the wake of the *Revolution,* but would be backed by the prosperous brokerage of Woodhull and Claflin and the generosity of Cornelius Vanderbilt.

From the beginning, the *Weekly* was a good-looking newspaper. In its opening pages, Woodhull tactfully paid her respects to the "brotherhood" of the press that she was joining, announcing "We think we have work to do, and we think a newspaper one of the means of doing that work." Installed as editor and given a weekly column,

Autograph of

Victoria C. Woodhull,
Future Presidentess

Beautiful handwriting
for formal correspon-
dence was the hallmark
of a good education in
19th-century America.
Woodhull attempted
to fulfill this self-
penned prophecy by
nominating herself for
President in 1870.

Stephen Pearl Andrews announced, "I have many things of immense importance which I want to communicate."

From her home in Murray Hill or in her office on Broad Street, Victoria Woodhull directed the business of the *Weekly*, often dictating editorials to Colonel Blood or to a staff of writers and editors. But she had not come to New York only to be a journalist, any more than she had come to be a broker. At 32 years of age, she had declared herself a candidate for the Presidency of the United States in order to argue for the equality of women with men and to urge a host of other widespread reforms. In the fall of 1870, with the *Weekly's* first few months of issues profitably off the press, Victoria Woodhull traveled to Washington to take her argument for woman suffrage to Congress.

CHAPTER

TAKING UP THE BURDEN: THE PETITIONER FOR WOMAN SUFFRAGE

Other speeches were made, but Woodhull had captured the committee, and the others were not needed.

—*The New York Herald*, January 13, 1871

Tireless campaigner Susan B. Anthony interrupted her cross-country lecture tour to go to Washington in January of 1871. A National Woman Suffrage Convention had been convened in the city, and Isabella Beecher Hooker, a younger sister in the celebrated Beecher family, had announced that she would finance, manage, and preside over the convention. Hooker told Anthony that she believed she might be able to restore the warring halves of the woman suffrage community into one whole. She supported the National Woman Suffrage Association led by the more militant and radical New York wing of Anthony and Stanton. But she also believed that her family connections would please the reformers from Boston, who were less willing to challenge the laws that limited women's rights and more willing to wait patiently for suffrage. Hooker's older sister, the educator and writer Catharine Beecher, was not convinced that women's suffrage would improve family life. She supported education for girls on the grounds that such education would improve their management of the household, which she believed was their proper sphere.

Another sister, Harriet Beecher Stowe, had brought home the horror of slavery to the nation in her novel *Uncle Tom's Cabin*. But Stowe had more recently published an account of the rebel poet Lord Byron that had shocked readers with its revelations of Byron's incestuous relationship with his half sister. With her account of Lord Byron, Stowe had put her own literary reputation at risk, and she was inclined now to make amends by looking askance at bold women's rights reformers. The most prominent of the Beecher siblings, Brooklyn preacher Henry Ward Beecher, was actually serving as the president of the Boston-based suffrage association. As for their sister, Bella Hooker, she was the wife of a distinguished abolitionist lawyer and the mother of three children. Who better than she, Isabella Beecher Hooker suggested to Susan B. Anthony, to lead the New York contingent's convention in Washington and restore the National Woman Suffrage Association to the prestige and dignity the Boston group believed it had lost?

But Susan B. Anthony had no intention of leaving all the managing to Isabella Beecher Hooker. She could not convince her dear friend and fellow campaigner Elizabeth Cady Stanton to interrupt her lecture tour to return to Washington, and so Anthony confronted alone the surprise that the convention had been hijacked, but not by Isabella Hooker.

The center of all the attention was Victoria Woodhull, about whom no one knew much. Woodhull had come to Washington earlier that fall, on a trip she had been planning for months. Even while she had been managing the *Weekly,* she had sent Tennie ahead as a scout to learn who were the power brokers behind the scenes in Congress. Woodhull had not forgotten the turmoil at the woman suffrage convention the year before. Under the tutelage of Colonel Blood and now Stephen Pearl Andrews, she meant to

Democratic and Republican candidates seek the support of the ordinary voter in Frank Leslie's 1888 political cartoon. At the voter's feet a temperance advocate, seeking to ban alcoholic beverages, offers the voter cold water, while woman suffragist Belva Lockwood, once a supporter of Victoria Woodhull, mounts a Presidential campaign of her own.

become an agent for political reform. The woman suffrage movement was divided and hard up for money. Stanton and Anthony were crisscrossing the country to lecture on women's rights to often hooting and hostile crowds. They were veterans of a twenty-year struggle and ready to embrace a second generation of rights leaders. Stanton had applauded Mrs. Hooker's offer to lead the Washington convention. "I am so glad to get anyone to take up the burden," she wrote to Anthony. "I say amen."

Woodhull came to Washington to bear just such a burden in the woman suffrage battle. She intended to take her argument directly to Congress, where a proposal for a 16th Amendment to enfranchise women had long been languishing in the House Judiciary Committee. Such a deathly dust was settling on the proposed 16th Amendment because the Republican administration of Ulysses S. Grant, although sympathetic, was reluctant to support the female suffrage cause. The Republicans had been the party of abolition, and enfranchisement would seem to many to be just as much the natural right of women as it was the natural right of black men. But Republicans were far more concerned with protecting the windfall they anticipated of some 2 million new black male voters enfranchised by the 14th and 15th Amendments. Among reformers, the abolition of slavery encouraged expectations that rights could be struggled for and won, but proponents of female suffrage were by no means a majority. If they supported female suffrage, reasoned many Republicans, they stood to lose more votes than they would gain.

Many prominent men, including journalists, ministers, and statesmen, argued that divine law itself opposed an active role for women in political life. Large numbers of women were themselves unconvinced that suffrage was desirable. Certainly not all middle-class women wanted to vote; they were happy to claim, like Catharine Beecher, that their sphere was the domestic one. Working-class women were more outspoken in backing economic reforms, wage equality, and improved working conditions than in pursuing equality at the voting booth. Although Anthony had been successful in forging some alliances between women's labor groups and the suffrage movement, working-class women believed that their more immediate interests lay elsewhere. These women were not always convinced that the ballot would put more bread on their table or improve the conditions of their labor. No surprise, then, that Republicans sympathetic to women's voting rights were not easily persuaded to raise the suffrage issue. Better all around, they thought, to let the 16th Amendment for woman suffrage die in committee.

Meanwhile, the 14th and 15th Amendments enfranchising black men had recently been ratified in state legislatures across the nation. During the rancorous convention of 1869, Victoria Woodhull had watched as the women's movement quarreled over its response to these amendments, draining its energies and financial resources by forming the two weakened camps in New York and Boston. The movement was riven, she wrote later in the *Humanitarian,* by "internal dissensions, divisions, and jealousies," which had been its bane from the beginning. Again her sympathies lay with the more radical wing that Stanton and Anthony led from New York. Like them, she did not believe that women should trade economic and political rights for dominion at home. Moreover, though she wanted suffrage and would lend the issue her voice and her money, she believed that women's social and economic independence was more important. As she wrote for the *Humanitarian,* "Her financial independence underlies all the rest."

Woodhull came to Washington with a plan. She had heard a proposal raised a year earlier by the Missouri suffragists Francis and Virginia Minor, who argued that the 14th and 15th Amendments to the Constitution, when properly understood, guaranteed suffrage to women as citizens of the United States as well as to black men. The 14th Amendment declared that all persons were citizens who were naturalized as citizens or born in the United States. The 15th Amendment barred states from denying the vote to citizens on the basis of race, color, or previous condition of servitude. Rather than seeking new constitutional amendments, the Minors' interpretation argued that women should demand the rights of suffrage at the polling places because these rights were already implied in the Constitution. Or women should use the courtrooms to challenge the state laws that barred them from voting. The Minors' proposal turned the suffrage campaign towards what has been called the "New Departure." Although Stanton briefly took up the campaign for a 16th Amendment enfranchising women, the argument that the Constitution already enfranchised women was the dominant suffrage strategy when Woodhull arrived in Washington.

In 1871, with the "New Departure" breathing fresh air into the suffrage movement, Victoria Woodhull opened up a second front. She took up the argument of the "New Departure" and broadened its applications. Rather than take her challenge to the courtroom, as the Minors would, she took her case to Congress itself, asking for a Declaratory Act that would affirm the right of all citizens to vote, including women. During the fall months of 1870, Woodhull had directed her campaign from Washington, using the *Weekly* in New York City as a vehicle for her message. In successive editorials through November and December, she called the proposed 16th Amendment "a dead letter." "I do now pro-

claim to the women of the United States of America," she
wrote, "that they are enfranchised."

In Washington, Woodhull sought out influential con-
gressmen whom she might lobby. She succeeded in
befriending Benjamin Butler, a short, pudgy, cigar-chomp-
ing Republican representative from Massachusetts. Butler
was a powerful political insider who had the ear and good-
will of President Grant, and he was hoping to lead his party
to victory under the banners of woman suffrage and labor
reform. He not only helped Woodhull draft her petition, he
intervened to obtain access for her to the House Judiciary
Committee, to which she submitted her "Memorial," as
petitions to Congress were called. By January 1871, the
women of the suffrage movement learned that the little-
known Victoria Woodhull had achieved an extraordinary
coup. She was going to present her petition on woman suffrage in the august chambers of Congress, where no woman
had ever spoken before.

Susan B. Anthony and Isabella Beecher Hooker heard
the news with stunned surprise. Hooker had only just come

*Victoria Woodhull
stands to read her
petition for female
suffrage to the Judiciary
Committee of the
House of Representa-
tives. Although
Woodhull was then
an inexperienced and
nervous speaker, one
newsman wrote, "If
her veins were opened
they would be found
to contain ice."*

from one woman to another as if he intended to select one of them for a wife." But when the chairman of the committee, John Bingham, suggested to Woodhull that she begin, there was no levity in her manner. She had never before addressed such an important audience, and when she rose to speak, she flushed deeply. Isabella Hooker thought Woodhull might faint. Instead she collected herself, and gradually her voice acquired strength. She spoke well, with a passion that carried deep conviction.

The Memorial she read that day was an amalgam of Stephen Pearl Andrews' belief that sovereignty belonged to each citizen and Benjamin Butler's insider strategy of reading closely the wording of the 14th and 15th Amendments. But the passion, conviction, and authority that Woodhull brought to her petition were hers, as was the simple triumph of having come from a wooden homestead on the Ohio frontier to stand now where far more fortunate women had been unable to appear.

Woodhull argued that political power is "not ever to be relinquished or abandoned" by anyone. She read a new meaning into the amendments that had only recently been written by the Congress she was addressing. Had not the 14th Amendment called native-born and naturalized persons "citizens"? Women were either native-born or naturalized. Had not the Congress forbidden denial of the vote on grounds of race, color, and previous condition of servitude? Women were of a race, possessed color, and, Woodhull pointed out, "from time immemorial groaned under what is properly termed in the Constitution 'previous condition of servitude.'" Making these arguments, Woodhull insisted that a woman's race and economic class shaped her life as much as did her gender, an important interpretation of the "New Departure."

Claiming that women's rights were as self-evident as men's, Woodhull also borrowed the sentimental picture of woman as wife and mother, an image that was being enshrined by her contemporaries as woman's separate and different divinely intended function. "They are entrusted with the most holy duties and the most vital responsibilities of society," said Woodhull. "They bear, rear, and educate men; they train and mould their characters; they inspire the noblest impulses in men . . ." But Woodhull spurned the compromise her sex seemed to have been offered—primacy at home if they would leave the public world to men. "It is by usurpation only," she argued, "that men debar them from their right to vote."

When she finished speaking, Woodhull gave the committee a courteous smile and bowed gracefully. The committee chair announced it would take time to consider their decision, but he looked impressed. One representative said Woodhull had presented her case "in as good style as any congressman could have done." "Other speeches were made," wrote the reporter for the *Herald,* "but Woodhull had captured the committee and others were not needed."

With her Memorial, Victoria Woodhull played an important role in the history of the "New Departure." In the first address by a woman to a congressional committee, she offered the "New Departure's" compelling argument for a reading of the Constitution that assured the natural rights of all citizens to the vote, a right that the federal government was sworn to protect. Furthermore, Woodhull assumed that the United States Congress, rather than the state legislatures or the courts, could be the solution to the woman suffrage question. Her petition to Congress reflected an apparent confidence in federal authority that was very much in the spirit of post–Civil War America. After all, the nation had just witnessed the federal government carrying the banner for human rights over the secessionist states of the South.

At the same time, Woodhull framed her Constitutional reading in a passionate moral rhetoric that would have pleased the suffragists who valued women's traditional roles as wife and mother even as they demanded the vote. Isabella Beecher Hooker now called her a womanly woman, her most precious accolade, and laid aside the warnings of her sisters Harriet and Catharine. Woodhull was not abandoning the argument of the sanctity of moral motherhood. She was willing to assume the moral superiority of women, as long as women could vote.

Anthony was exultant at the "New Departure's" shift of focus from the state to the national government. "Good can come out of Washington," Anthony told a *Herald* reporter. "The national capital shall yet be the glory of her sex and all the rest of man and womankind." The *Herald* agreed. "There is no disguising the fact that the woman suffrage advocates are making headway in Washington."

When the House Judiciary Committee adjourned, both Hooker and Anthony welcomed Victoria Woodhull to the sisterhood of suffrage workers. They brought her to Lincoln Hall that afternoon for the opening meeting of the suffrage convention, and bade her repeat her Memorial to the audience. Hooker wrote to Savery, "She was very nervous at first. I was by her; she swayed to and fro, and I thought she would fall. She collected herself, and delivered it very well."

Woodhull had become the talk of Washington. Even Horace Greeley's anti-suffrage newspaper the *Tribune,* which heaped sarcasm and sneers upon the convention, acknowledged Woodhull as a new leader. President Ulysses S. Grant invited Woodhull to the White House. Gesturing to his own armchair, he told her flatteringly, but perhaps not sincerely, "Someday you will occupy that chair."

Neither the President nor the House Judiciary Committee proved a steady friend. On January 30, the committee rejected Woodhull's petition. The phrase "a citizen of the United States . . . means nothing more nor less than a member of the nation," opined the Committee. It was the prerogative of individual states, the report continued, to extend the privilege of franchise. The committee did not accept Woodhull's argument that women were included in the phrase "race, color, or previous condition of servitude."

By the same logic, suggested the committee, underage and non-resident citizens could appeal to states to be enfranchised. Benjamin Butler wrote a lengthy minority opinion a few weeks later supporting Woodhull. But the House Judiciary Committee's decision was ultimately upheld in a test case brought to the Supreme Court by Virginia Minor four years later. In *Minor v. Happerstat* the Court ruled in 1875 that citizenship did not imply the right to vote. The power to enfranchise was left to the individual states, unless the federal government could be persuaded to amend the Constitution once again.

Isabella Beecher Hooker, the youngest daughter in the prominent Beecher family, was an active female suffragist and passionate believer in the existence of spirits. One New Year's Eve she assembled a group of friends to await the descent of spirit visitors who would invest Hooker with special powers to create a woman-centered government.

The Judiciary Committee's rejection of Woodhull's petition in no way deflated her ascendancy in the suffrage movement. She rented Lincoln Hall in Washington for another meeting and printed impressive pamphlets advertising addresses on "Constitutional Equality, Legal and Moral Views." She suggested that she might donate more money, perhaps as much as $10,000. The meeting secured Woodhull's place in the leadership of the movement. When Isabella Beecher Hooker took joint billing with her as a cosponsor, the acid-tongued *Tribune* remarked that "the Beecher-Hooker branch of the party, the most conservative of all as regards matrimony, marches on to victory or death behind the editor of a journal remarkable principally for its lax views upon such questions."

Others beside Hooker stood with Victoria Woodhull. Paulina Wright Davis rose to present Woodhull to the great

continued on page 72

WE MEAN TREASON

Several weeks after presenting her Memorial on woman suffrage to the United States Congress in 1871, Victoria Woodhull delivered "A Lecture on Congressional Equality" in Washington. In this extract from her lecture, Woodhull demanded the vote as a right of citizenship, winning the admiration of the movement's leadership and helping to steer the suffrage campaign in a new direction.

If Congress refuse to listen to and grant what women ask, there is but one course left them to pursue. Women have no government. Men have organized a government, and they maintain it to the utter exclusion of women. Women are as much members of the nation as men are, and they have the same human right to govern themselves which men have. Men have none but an usurped right to the arbitrary control of women. Shall free, intelligent, reasoning, thinking women longer submit to being robbed of their common rights. Men fashioned a government based on their own enunciation of principles: that taxation without representation is tyranny; and that all just government exists by the consent of the governed. Proceeding upon *these* axioms, they formed a Constitution declaring all persons to be citizens, that one of the rights of a citizen is the right to vote, and that no power within the nation shall either make or enforce laws interfering with the citizen's rights. And yet men deny women the first and greatest of all the rights of citizenship, the right to vote.

Under such glaring inconsistencies, such unwarrantable tyranny, such unscrupulous despotism, what is there left women to do but to become the mothers of the future government.

We *will* have our rights. We say no longer by your leave, we have besought, argued and convinced, but we have failed; *and we will not fail.* We will try you *just once more.* If the very next Congress refuse women all the legitimate results of citizenship; if they indeed merely so much as fail by a proper declaratory act to withdraw every obstacle to the most ample exercise of the franchise, then we give here and now, deliberate notification of what we will do next.

There is one alternative left, and we have resolved on that. This convention is for the purpose of this declaration. As surely as one year passes from this day, and this right is not fully, frankly and unequivocally considered, we shall proceed to call another convention expressly to frame a new constitution and to erect a new government, complete in all its parts, and to take measures to maintain it as effectually as men do theirs.

If for people to govern themselves is so unimportant a matter as men now assert it to be, they could not justify themselves in interfering. If, on the contrary, it is the important thing we conceive it to be, they can but applaud us for exercising our right.

We mean treason; we mean secession, and on a thousand times grander scale than was that of the South. We are plotting revolution; we will overslough this bogus republic and plant a government of righteousness in its stead, which shall not only profess to derive its power from the consent of the governed, but shall do so in reality.

We rebel against, denounce and defy this arbitrary, usurping and tyrannical government which has been framed and imposed on us without our consent, and even without so much as entertaining the idea that it was or could be of the slightest consequence what we should think of it, or how our interests should be affected by it, or even that we existed at all except in the simple case in which we might be found guilty of some offense against its behests, when it has not failed to visit on us its sanctions with as much rigor as if we owed rightful allegiance to it; which we do not, and which, in the future, we will not even pretend to do.

continued from page 69

crowd in the Lincoln Hall assembly, where latecomers found only standing room. Davis echoed the militancy of the "New Departure," telling the audience that women did not merely ask for suffrage but now demanded it.

When Woodhull spoke, she reminded the Lincoln assembly of the noble protests of "no taxation without representation" that had launched the American Revolution a century earlier. "I am subject to tyranny. I am taxed in every conceivable way . . . I do now claim that I am, equally with men, possessed of the right to vote, and if no others of my sex claim it, I will stand alone." Elizabeth Cady Stanton telegraphed her approval from her lecture tour. "We who pay millions in taxes propose to be something more than members of the nation," she wrote, dismissing as insulting the description of citizenship with which the Judiciary Committee had rejected Woodhull's petition.

Stanton had harbored some misgivings that the "New Departure" would be a less successful strategy for suffrage than pursuit of a 16th Amendment. But she wrote Woodhull in February 1871 that her mind "was set to rest at that point" by the show of support from important Republicans such as Benjamin Butler. Susan B. Anthony resumed her own lecture tour with a freshly written speech that abandoned demands for a 16th Amendment and instead called on women everywhere to go to the polls and demand to vote.

Woodhull had been launched. She left Washington to speak at public meetings in New York, Boston, and Philadelphia. She met and won the support of the Quaker abolitionist Lucretia Mott, who, with Stanton, had convened the first women's rights conference some 30 years earlier. Benjamin Butler's encouraging comment that she had the makings of a great orator buoyed her. In New York City in May, confident and animated, Woodhull refined her message for another important suffrage meeting. The news-

papers now gave her top billing. Sitting next to her on the platform in Apollo Hall were her familiar companions from Washington, now including Elizabeth Cady Stanton, who had returned from her lecture tour. The *Herald* headlined these venerable figures as "Woodhull's women." Stanton was so certain that the vote was at hand that she directed her remarks to those improvements that would ensure that men and women would vote well. Susan B. Anthony herself introduced Victoria Woodhull at the New York meeting. Woodhull was, said Anthony, the first representative of Wall Street who had ever appeared on a suffrage platform. Here, suggested Anthony, was someone pouring the lifeblood of the New York Stock Exchange into the suffrage movement.

Now there was no nervous pallor or flushing and near-fainting when Victoria Woodhull rose to speak. Assuming

The mid-19th-century meeting places where middle class women addressed current social reform issues often resembled private drawing rooms. The background of a domestic interior softened the widespread opinion that women orators publicly disgraced their fathers or husbands.

73

her mantle as an important spokesperson for the suffrage movement, Woodhull adopted the militant politics of Stephen Pearl Andrews, ideas in the revolutionary lineage of the Declaration of Independence. She argued that no one could take her rights from her. They belonged to her, not to the government. If Congress refuses us again, she told the Apollo Hall convention, "we will make a new Constitution and erect a new government." "We mean treason," she proclaimed. "We mean secession, and on a thousand times grander scale than was that of the South. We denounce this arbitrary government imposed upon us without our consent." She promised the convention that although she was a candidate for the Presidency, "I have no personal ambition. I do all to advance the interests of humanity."

After the New York convention, the luminaries departed. Anthony and Stanton left to ride the rails again across the country, taking the message about woman suffrage to midland cities and frontier towns. Before they left, the women heaped upon Woodhull the sweet words of welcome to their sisterhood. Susan B. Anthony kept to herself for the moment some concerns that Woodhull's passion for the suffrage might be less single-minded than her own and could be mixed with more personal ambition than she admitted.

As for rumors that Woodhull trailed a questionable past and a disreputable family, Anthony scoffed in a March letter to suffragist Martha Coffin Wright: "When we women begin to search individual records and antecedents of those who bring influence, brains, and cash to our work of enfranchising woman—we shall begin with the men." Meanwhile she did not hesitate to find ways to loosen Woodhull's purse strings for the cause of suffrage. Joyously she wrote to Woodhull, "Go ahead! Bright, glorious, young, and strong spirit, and believe in the best love, and hope and faith of Susan B. Anthony."

Isabella Beecher Hooker wrote rapturously to Woodhull in the effusive style common among women friends at the time, calling her "my darling Queen." "You are fitted for political strife and a pure leadership, I firmly believe," she wrote. "I give you my blessing and deepest sympathy and warmest prayers." In the enthusiasm of her new friendship, Mrs. Hooker allowed only one misgiving to surface. As she planned the May convention in New York City with Woodhull, she was chagrined to discover that the call to the meeting promised discussion of "social questions" as well as suffrage. Writing back to Woodhull, Hooker advised against this inclusion and hesitated to sign her name to the call. "We can afford to wait for discussions of social questions till we are the political equals of men."

Isabella Beecher Hooker and most of her suffragist sisters—though not Elizabeth Cady Stanton—adamantly preferred that the conditions of women's private lives not be raised. Others worried that women who might otherwise have flocked to the suffrage banner would be deterred by the controversy that would be raised by discussing birth control or challenging marriage laws. Hooker's hopes for silence on the "social questions" would soon be dramatically and conclusively dashed.

The novelist Harriet Beecher Stowe stood loyally by her brother, the prominent minister Henry Ward Beecher, when he was accused of adultery. Stowe said that Victoria Woodhull, whose revelations about Beecher fanned the fires of the scandal, was "a snake and should be given a good clip with a shovel."

4

ROCKING THE BOAT: THE "SOCIAL QUESTIONS"

*The men and women who are dabbling with the suffrage move-
ment for women should be at once therefore and emphatically
warned what they mean logically if not consciously in all they say
is next social equality, and next Freedom, or in a word Free Love,
and if they wish to get out of the boat, they should for safety get
out now, for delays are dangerous.*

—Elizabeth Cady Stanton, "On Marriage and Divorce"

The person who first linked Victoria Woodhull to the scandalous notion of "free love" was her own mother. In May
1871, Annie Claflin was an angry and unbalanced woman.
For a long while, she had resented Colonel Blood for, as
she saw it, spiriting both her daughters away from the family
business of fortune-telling and healing. Now she was convinced that the Colonel was stealing money from her Vicky
and Tennie while he managed the brokerage and the
Weekly. Rich as her girls were, Annie felt they all could be
richer still, even riding in their own carriages down Fifth
Avenue. Many nights Annie screamed curses at Blood in
the parlor of the 38th-Street mansion where she, Buck, and
other Claflin kin had taken up residence. She would see

him in the penitentiary, she yelled, and he would end his life there. Coming upon her in this state, Woodhull and Tennie would hustle their mother away. As for the imperturbable Blood, interrupted in his bookkeeping, he confessed that had she not been his mother-in-law he would have liked to spank her.

Only a few days after her daughter's triumphant speech at Apollo Hall, Annie Claflin took her revenge. She brought a criminal complaint against Colonel Blood, charging him with threatened assault and with alienating the affections of her daughters. Woodhull's hope that the court case might be hushed up died quickly. Instead, for several days the embarrassing quarrels of the huckstering, vagabonding, low-life Claflins were played out in the crowded Essex Street Police Court, then served up for the delight of the newspaper-reading public in New York City. "The Woodhull War" headlined the *Herald,* which only weeks earlier had more respectfully chronicled Woodhull's successes.

Poor Annie, toothless and with her country accent, made amusing copy for the journalists as she protested that her son-in-law claimed he would wash his hands in her blood. Though she did not see Colonel Blood to the penitentiary nor win back her daughters to a life of fortune-telling, her poisonous words wreaked a havoc beyond any success she might have imagined. Far more interesting than Colonel Blood's alleged violent threats was her description of the household on 38th Street, which the *Herald* printed verbatim: "S'help me God, Judge," she testified to the delight of the spectators and journalists packing the courtroom, "I say here and I call Heaven to witness that there was the worst gang of free lovers in that house in 38th street that ever lived—Stephen Pearl Andrews and Dr. Woodhull and lots more of such trash."

"Spicy revelations," crowed the *Herald.* "A very Happy and Unique Family," their headlines observed with amusement. Not only had Annie Claflin disclosed that her daughter's former husband still found shelter in their household, but, even more calamitously, she had attached the doctrine of "free love" to Victoria Woodhull. For years, those hostile to reform had sought to ridicule or revile women advocating their own rights by calling them "old maids" or, if they criticized the institution of marriage, "free lovers" whose abandonment of conventional morality put them beyond the pale of serious consideration. Now Woodhull's own mother was showing how Victoria Woodhull could be mocked, reproved, and discarded.

In the reform-minded years after the Civil War, everyone had heard of free love, but few knew precisely what it meant. Decades earlier, the reformer John Humphrey Noyes had first coined the term when he preached a form of "Bible communism" and multiple marriages in his utopian Oneida community in upstate New York. Stephen Pearl Andrews had rejected state laws governing marriage at his community Modern Times, believing, as had many social revolutionary figures before him, that the state had no business regulating the most intimate relations of a citizen's life.

But the free-love movement was by no means confined to the utopian dreamers on the eastern seaboard who planned experimental communities. The movement took root as well in small farming towns of the Midwest, where radical reformers demanded open and frank discussions of sexuality, its place in married life, and the benefits to society of improved sexual education.

Free love might mean anything from the right to form close friendships to the right to promiscuous sexual relations. Certainly anyone advocating reform of the laws that regulated marriage might be called a "free lover." Many religious and civic leaders believed that these laws were the underpinnings of social stability. They regarded the rising divorce rate and the demand for women's rights as threats to the traditional authority embodied in the rights of a husband—his rights to his wife's property, to her children, and to her body, with or without her consent. These laws had long been anathema to some reformers in the women's rights movement. Women were rendered not only economically dependent by them, they argued, but also, with contraception not widely available, women were helpless to control their own reproductive life. With such laws in place, women's hopes for an autonomous adult life were severely limited.

Among the women's rights advocates, Elizabeth Cady Stanton had long been willing to challenge the legal constraints that denied women freedom in marriage. Foremost among these abuses was the longstanding legal opinion that because a husband had full title to his wife's property, his ownership included sexual rights to her body as well. Law clerks routinely learned the phrase "the right of property in the wife," which permitted a husband to force sexual intercourse with his wife. Victorian moralists often called such violence unnatural and barbaric, but they did not call it rape.

When Stanton toured the country to speak about woman suffrage, she held private meetings at night for wives. She was struck by the premature aging of the young women she met in the plains and in the new settlements of the western territories. Here were young 16-year-old mothers, for whom marriage meant uninterrupted pregnancies, failing health, and often shortened lives. In those evening meetings in small communities across the United States, Stanton talked about birth control and a woman's unalienable right to be sovereign over her own body. Earlier, Stanton had criticized the double standard of sexual morality that forgave men's adulteries but not women's. Now she turned to the marriage laws themselves. In May 1870, Stanton told a mixed-sex New York meeting that though she had worked all her life for woman suffrage, "My future word should be to teach woman her duties to herself in the home." "What is wanted," she argued "is freedom from all unnecessary entanglements and concessions, freedom from binding obligations involving impossibilities, freedom to repair mistakes." In fact, Stanton wanted "unlimited freedom of divorce, freedom to institute at the option of the parties new amatory relationships, love put above marriage, and in a word the obnoxious doctrine of Free Love. Well, yes, that is what I mean," she told her audience. "We are one and all free lovers at heart."

When she seemed to encourage women to leave unhappy marriages, Stanton found her audiences shrinking. With little education and few opportunities for earning their own way, women were often unwilling to see the weakening of marriage laws that allowed, for example, divorce in New York State only on grounds of adultery. Many women wholly dependent on their husbands' income worried that with divorce laws made easier, they would be abandoned to poverty. Wishing to enlist as many women as possible into her campaign for marriage reform and suffrage, Stanton was careful to save her advocacy of free love for sympathetic audiences. Though she supported unlimited freedom of divorce to enable new, loving relationships to form, she assumed that such relationships would be monogamous. Other free love advocates permitted multiple relationships.

As for Victoria Woodhull, her disastrous first marriage had long before convinced her that traditional marriage was no security for financial or emotional well-being. But although she was a ready pupil for Stephen Pearl Andrews' teachings, she had not chosen to make such "social questions" her political platform. She had begun her Presidential campaign as a suffragist, and even as Annie Claflin brought her suit she was preparing speeches on labor and finance issues. Now, with Annie's artless revelations, she was compelled to acknowledge how much more profoundly she would be willing to challenge notions of propriety.

On May 20, several days after the *Herald* trumpeted the "astonishing revelations by old Mrs. Claflin," Woodhull defended her living arrangements in a letter to the *New York Times*. "Dr. Woodhull being sick, ailing, and incapable of self support, I felt it my duty to myself and to human nature that he should be cared for." Colonel Blood, she wrote, accepted and approved of such human charity. Moreover, she reminded the *Times's* readers, she was and had been a married woman. "I live in one house with one who was my husband; I live as the wife with one who is my husband." "I believe in Spiritualism," she acknowledged. "I advocate free love in the highest, purest sense, as the only cure for the immorality, the deep damnation by which men corrupt and disfigure God's most truly holy institution of sexual relations."

Cartoonist Thomas Nast portrays Victoria Woodhull as Mrs. Satan, promoting free love and luring a loyal wife away from her drunkard husband. Woodhull argued, "Where there is no love as a basis of marriage, there should be no marriage!"

Furthermore, Woodhull wrote, those men who presumed to judge her "preach against 'free love' openly and practice it secretly." In Washington, she had heard the gossip about the brother of Isabella Beecher Hooker, the Reverend Henry Ward Beecher, now a portly and comfortable man of 60 years. Beecher's sermons filled the expensive pews at Plymouth Church in Brooklyn and raised the value of its property. Beecher had lent abolition his powerful voice, but he was not among the first to embrace this reform. He was not a courageous advocate for social change, for he was reluctant to stir troubled waters and risk offending the financial backers who owned bonds in the profitable tax-free property of the church.

Woodhull believed Beecher was guilty of moral hypocrisy, preaching a morality he did not practice. Referring to Beecher, Woodhull wrote in her letter to the *Times,* "I know of one man, a public teacher of eminence, who lives in concubinage with the wife of another public teacher of almost equal eminence." She would not, she proclaimed, be the object of public ridicule while powerful men privately flouted the same social conventions that she was scorned for challenging.

In her letter, Woodhull was declaring her allegiances. Invoking spiritualism, she linked herself with that religious awakening that had grown up outside established churches and beyond the reaches of traditional religious constraints on sexuality. The notion of free love that she espoused was a familiar notion among spiritualists, who believed that a love derived from God would purify human relationships.

But with her veiled reference to Henry Ward Beecher, Victoria Woodhull was taking on powerful adversaries. Because Beecher was a money-maker for bankers and merchants who knew he could command large audiences, they would not see his reputation tarnished by a whiff of scandal. Nor was infidelity in a man considered so very reprehensible, as long as he behaved himself discreetly. The double standard of sexual morality permitted such dalliance in men, as long as social standards were not publicly challenged. To be sure, some utopian communities had publicly experimented with multiple marriages, but they were understood to be odd societies beyond the city squares. Woodhull's impressive mansion on 38th Street, with its imposing architectural facade, stood in the heartland of affluent New York City. It would be bad enough for a man from such a house to proclaim free love from its rooftop, but that a woman should make such an announcement offered a serious challenge to sacred and sentimental notions of femininity.

Reading about the Claflin scandal and the letter to the *Times,* Woodhull's newly won friends in the suffrage movement were at first reassuring. Paulina Wright Davis wrote to her that she believed Woodhull was "raised up by God" to "unmask the hypocrisy of a class that none others dare touch." The more she thought of that "mass of Beecher corruption," the more she longed for Woodhull to lance the infection.

Woodhull also received a long, sympathetic letter from Elizabeth Cady Stanton, written as Stanton's train headed toward Wyoming Territory, where the legislature had recently given women the right to vote. Stanton greeted Woodhull as "the last victim sacrificed on the altar of woman's suffrage." "All this low gossiping about the blunders of your childhood and the sorrows of your maturer years," she raged. The editors were crushing Woodhull, she wrote, because "they hated the principles of equality" and would not answer the "able" argument of Woodhull's Memorial to Congress.

But the reaction in the suffrage camp was not all favorable. Susan B. Anthony was silent, reading letters from a close friend who urged suffrage leaders to "refute" the "falsehood" that "we have all gone over to free love." Only a month earlier, suffragist Sarah Stearns had embraced Woodhull at the May convention, offering a resolution to commend her "courage, independence of character, her liberality and high moral worth." Now she wrote that she would not easily find women willing to work or give money "so long as Mrs. Woodhull's connection" with the movement was not explained. "I would like to have the name of Victoria C. Woodhull, as connected with Women's Suffrage, as soon forgotten as possible."

Indeed, in the months that followed the embarrassing court testimony at the Essex Street Police Station, Woodhull had not allowed the free love accusation to die quietly, as her suffrage coworkers had hoped. She chose instead to debate the philosophy of free love in the newspapers, perhaps to divert attention from her unconventional household and her unruly relatives.

Another means of rescuing her public reputation came to hand when Theodore Tilton, the widely respected reform leader and journalist, came to Woodhull's door. Tilton was not only a woman suffrage advocate, he was a handsome, fair-haired man with a classical profile that

Theodore Tilton was a popular journalist, lecturer, and reform advocate when he befriended Victoria Woodhull. A handsome man, he was described as a "perfect Adonis with whom any woman of sentiment would fall in love."

looked as if it should be cast in marble. As a young man, he had become a good friend and protégé of Henry Ward Beecher, who had blessed the Tiltons' marriage. Away frequently on lecture tours, Tilton believed that his wife and Beecher, their minister, had become lovers, but he was reluctant to drag his family through scandal with an accusation. Moreover, he needed Beecher's support to advance his own career as a journalist. For the time, Tilton lay aside his jealous rage and sought out Victoria Woodhull to persuade her to be silent as well.

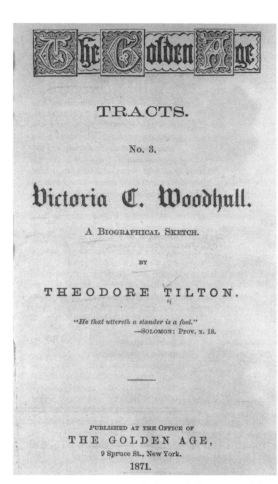

Theodore Tilton's
admiring biographical
sketch of Victoria
Woodhull helped to
win the support of the
spiritualist community
for her Presidential
nomination. The biog-
raphy stated that
Woodhull "entertained
angels" who "dictate
her life with daily
revelation."

Tilton befriended Woodhull. In the course of a long summer, he wrote a star-struck biography of her that suggested to many that they had become intimate. Although he was not himself inclined to believe in spirits, Tilton undertook a defense of Woodhull's notion of free love that reminded his readers that "she is a spiritualist of the most mystical and ethereal type."

As she developed a defense of free love over the summer of 1871, Woodhull described its practice in the vocabulary of spiritualism. What she loathed, she wrote to abolitionist reformer Gerrit Smith, were "secret vices," which were sexual relations without love. These "undermine human happiness," she explained. Like other spiritualists, Woodhull believed that moral love was possible only when lovers were united by God-given natural impulses. If not founded in love, sexual relations within marriage led to an unhealthy and unhappy society in which purely physical impulses reigned. Alcoholism in men and nervous diseases in women, she believed, were the outcomes of such debased unions.

In the fall of 1871, the sensational death in New York City of a young woman by illegal abortion gave Woodhull an opportunity to expand her argument that linked marriage law to societal ill health. Abortion, though not sanctioned by law, was widely practiced in New York City in the late 19th century, with expensive physicians for the rich and back-alley provisions for the poor. In the *Weekly,* Woodhull indicted the hypocrisy that tolerated this system, a convenience not only for the "thousand gentlemen within the purlieus of Wall Street" who seek out these services, but also for "the married women among the wealthy."

These wealthy women, argued Woodhull, were quite unlike the mothers so sentimentally beloved by popular illustrators and writers. Instead they were leading dissipated and senseless lives. In fact "the oppressions and disgust of the marriage state; their hopeless and aimless lives; all together have so depressed the nervous energy of our women that they dread beyond endurance the burdens and the care of children. They have become unfit to have children, and abortion is the sewerage for this wretched stagna-

Harriet Beecher Stowe savagely mocked Victoria Woodhull in her novel My Wife and I. *Imagining Woodhull as the unscrupulous and seductive Audacia Dangyereyes, Stowe describes her boldly accosting men in their business offices to solicit subscriptions to her newspaper.*

FREE SPEECH, FREE LOVE

In her pathbreaking public lecture of November 1871, "The Principles of Social Freedom," Victoria Woodhull joined many 19th-century reformers who believed that civil laws regulating marriage and divorce violated the spirit of the American Revolution as enshrined in the Bill of Rights. Condemning women's having to marry for economic security, Woodhull declared a right to love freely.

Two persons, a male and a female, meet, and are drawn together by a mutual attraction—a natural feeling unconsciously arising within their natures of which neither has any control—which is denominated love. This is a matter that concerns these two, and no other living soul has any human right to say aye, yes, or no, since it is a matter in which none except the two have any right to be involved, and from which it is the duty of these two to exclude every other person, since no one can love for another or determine why another loves . . . At no point in the process designated has there been any other than an exercise of the right of the two individuals to pursue happiness in their own way, which way has neither crossed nor interfered with any one else's right to the same pursuit; therefore, there is no call for a law to change, modify, protect or punish this exercise. It must be concluded then, if individuals have the Constitutional right to pursue happiness in their own way, that all compelling laws of marriage and divorce are despotic, being remnants of the barbaric ages in which they were origi-nated, and utterly unfitted for an age so advanced upon that, and so enlightened in the general principles of freedom and equality as is this . . . To love is a right higher than Constitutions or laws. It is a right which Constitutions and laws can neither give nor take, and with which they have nothing whatever to do, since in its very nature it is forever independent of both Constitutions and laws, and exists—comes and goes—in spite of them.

tion of feminine life." Woodhull insisted on sexual education for both men and women, deploring particularly that the young girl is "kept in ignorance by her own mother." To deny such education would lead to abuse and promiscuity. Woodhull insisted that "the freedom to be healthy must be absolute."

Having spent the summer and early fall rehearsing her arguments in the *Weekly* and in correspondence, Woodhull prepared to deliver one of the most important speeches of her public life, a discourse on "social freedoms." Meanwhile, her veiled threats about Beecher had not gone unnoticed. The Beecher sisters Catharine and Harriet rallied

"AND THE TRUTH SHALL MAKE YOU FREE."

A SPEECH

ON THE

Principles of Social Freedom,

DELIVERED IN

STEINWAY HALL, MONDAY, NOVEMBER 20, 1871,

AND

MUSIC HALL, BOSTON, WEDNESDAY, JANUARY 3, 1872,

And to Audiences of Thousands throughout the United States.

BY

VICTORIA CLAFLIN WOODHULL

(MRS. JOHN BIDDULPH MARTIN.)

LONDON ·
BLACKFRIARS PRINTERS, LIMITED,
8, SALISBURY COURT, FLEET STREET, E.C.
1894.

around their brother. Harriet Beecher Stowe pilloried Woodhull as the fictional character "Miss Audacia Dangyereyes" in a satirical novel called *My Wife and I,* which ran successfully in installments in the *Christian Union* newspaper, Henry Ward Beecher's publication. In a vain attempt by younger sister Isabella to reconcile her family to her new friend, Catharine Beecher, now past seventy, traveled to New York to drive Woodhull around Central Park in her carriage. According to Woodhull later, the meeting did not go well: Catharine had raised her fist to Woodhull, promising to strike her dead if she spoke out against Henry.

But Isabella Beecher Hooker remained loyal to Woodhull. In a long letter to Anna Savery, she confided that "Some of her messages seem unwise and unchristian. But never has her motive or general drift of thought

Woodhull's history-making speech, reprinted in London almost a quarter century later, was a defense of free love. Although by then she denied ever having advocated free love, one former friend claimed, "every person who was intimately acquainted with Victoria C. Woodhull in the early 70s is sure that . . . she was in ardent sympathy with every word of it."

seemed other than the purest and highest I can conceive." Writing in November 1871, Hooker was moved by Woodhull's loyal and benevolent care of Canning Woodhull and her kind mothering of the unfortunate mentally damaged Byron. A profound believer in spirits herself, Hooker accepted Woodhull as a "prophetess, full of visions and messages," but, she wrote to Savery, "it is dreadful this having foes in your own household," she conceded, thinking of sisters Harriet and Catharine.

On Woodhull's part, as she rented the largest hall in New York City for her speech, she sought out Henry Ward Beecher and offered him a compromise. She would hold her tongue about his love affairs if he would stand by her side and introduce her when she spoke on social freedoms in November. By so doing, he would make public that he accepted the free love ideas he was practicing. According to the account later published in the *Weekly,* Beecher knelt at her feet, weeping and begging to be let off. He could not endure the public disgrace that would ensue, he pleaded, and would take his own life before submitting to disgrace. Finally the distraught Beecher promised to try to gather his courage and do as she asked at Steinway Hall.

In the end, Beecher did not show up, but Victoria Woodhull did not name him. With rain coming down in torrents on the evening of November 20, it seemed that half of New York was willing to pay their fifty cents to hear Victoria Woodhull speak on "The Principles of Social Freedom." Three thousand people crowded into the auditorium—respectable merchants and their wives, street-walkers and ruffians, all jostling elbows—while in the lobby a small boy collected a fee for checking their dripping umbrellas. Various Claflin kin found seats in the balcony and at the sides of the stage, while Woodhull and her sister Tennessee conferred in a nearby passageway and waited for the errant Beecher. As the *Herald* described the evening, Stephen Pearl Andrews found his seat, calling out "God Speed!" to

Woodhull where she waited. Still Beecher did not arrive. Finally Theodore Tilton leapt to his feet. "Are you going to introduce Mrs. Woodhull to the audience?" cried out a friend. "Yes by heaven," said Tilton, "since no one else has the pluck to do it."

A great cry came up from the audience when Victoria Woodhull, wearing a black suit and a tea rose at her throat, walked onto the stage. The audience was prepared for a riveting evening. Part spectacle, part instruction, such lectures were by no means solemn events. Before radio, movies, and television, public lectures were a great national form of entertainment. The men and women had come in out of the rain to cheer or to hiss, to call out rude questions or to shout approval.

With great clarity and care, Woodhull laid out the principles she had been rehearsing, a heady compounded dose of Stephen Pearl Andrews's notion of individual sovereignty and a spiritualist's notion of love. Governments served only to protect the rights that belong to the people. Citizens could no more be denied their social freedoms than they could be denied their political and religious freedoms. As for this social freedom, it was the exercise of "God's natural law" that compelled two people to love, not man's law. All marriage laws were, therefore, a tyranny, because love took its authority from nature, not from the courts. To marry for economic reasons, as women's dependency so often led them to do, was sinful. To live as a wife to a husband without love—merely because he provided economic support—was prostitution.

The audience was by turns stunned into silence or roused to hissing and stomping. When one or two gentlemen seated in the front of the house shouted out a hostile comment, Woodhull cordially invited them to exercise their rights to free speech alongside her on stage. Another noisy heckler was revealed as a Claflin, an older sister of Woodhull's who clambered onto the stage to share the limelight and was persuaded gently to leave. With the audience hurling noisy derision, Woodhull at first shrank back, but then came boldly forward to utter words that made newspaper headlines across the country. "Yes, I am a free lover," she claimed defiantly. "I have an inalienable, constitutional and natural right to love whom I may, to love as long or as short a period as I can, to change that love every day if I please, and with that right neither you nor any law you can frame have any right to interfere." With her bold affirmation, Victoria Woodhull raised the banner of free love, claiming its most radical meaning: the right to love as often as one pleased. Few people at Steinway Hall that night would forget the courage of the slim woman standing alone, daring to hold her most private life inviolate against legislatures and courtrooms.

The evening ended well. The newspapers, even Horace Greeley's *Tribune,* acknowledged that she had spoken eloquently. Those who had come to Steinway Hall expecting to be repulsed by vulgarity had been disappointed. Woodhull had explained her beliefs with dignity and founded them in a profoundly moral vision of individual integrity and social well-being. She had denied that chaos or promiscuity would assail the social order, and promised that a healthier, happier society would follow this freedom as it had followed political and religious freedoms.

Elizabeth Cady Stanton, who had been working for the reform of marriage laws long before Victoria Woodhull, was buoyed by the fervor of Woodhull's speech and the relatively respectful reception it drew. For the first time in American public life, it seemed to Stanton and to others, it was possible to talk about sexual life candidly. Almost 100 years before twentieth-century feminists declared that "the personal is political," Stanton recognized with Woodhull that women's political freedoms could not be won without reforming the conditions of their private lives. Stanton had written in 1870 that suffrage was only the first step to women's emancipation. "Next is social equality." If the words "free love" frightened people, then she warned them that they should "get out of the boat now."

Still, there were auguries of storms to come. Henry Ward Beecher had not stood by Woodhull's side that night at Steinway Hall. He had not admitted that he reserved for himself a freedom in his private life that he denied when he mounted the pulpit. Moreover, many in the woman suffrage movement would "get out of the boat" rather than share space with the woman who was becoming known as "the" Woodhull. Catharine Beecher had leaned out of her carriage and darkly threatened her. It remained to be seen if Victoria Woodhull could indeed expose the hypocrisy of important men without bringing down their vengeance on her own head.

Woodhull and Claflin's elegantly printed newspaper was one of many 19th-century written works made possible by cheaper paper and more efficient printing processes that increased maximum production from 300 sheets per day to 15,000 sheets per hour. The Weekly's editor, Stephen Pearl Andrews, told subscribers the Weekly was "a sort of walking university, going about all over the country; coming into your parlors and workshops and kitchens; settling the great questions of government and labor and life."

5

PARTING THE RED SEA: ON THE CAMPAIGN TRAIL

She has opened the Red Sea before us who were willing to pass through under her leadership.

—Isabella Beecher Hooker to Elizabeth Cady Stanton, May 12, 1872

After her Steinway Hall speech on marriage reform, Woodhull received a flood of invitations to lecture, many offering fees that were welcome revenue for the coffers of the brokerage firm of Woodhull and Claflin. In fact, the firm was not prospering. The sisters had been speculating unwisely in the unstable gold market, and several clients, seeing their investments shrink, had closed their accounts. Woodhull was not alone in suffering the sudden reversals of industrial capitalism. In 1871, the economy was on the eve of one of the great depressions of the 19th century. These crises occurred with such alarming regularity that they seemed inseparable from the system of free enterprise itself, leaving many small businesses ruined and hungry working people helpless in the cycles of profit and loss.

Here was a clash between workers and bosses that Woodhull prepared herself to enter. Although she may have begun her Presidential campaign, as she said herself, only to bring attention to those reforms she espoused, by now Victoria Woodhull was taking her Presidential campaign more seriously. Others saw her as a spokesperson for Stephen Pearl Andrews or perhaps for the Republican representative Benjamin Butler, who had helped her bring her Memorial to Congress. But she saw herself as a standard-bearer for a broad base of reforms by no means limited to the "social questions" the newspapers had enjoyed featuring. Although she may never have imagined herself actually elected to the White House, she sensed her power as a shaper of public opinion, so long as the newspapers regarded her as good copy and audiences filled her lecture halls. She sought now to broaden her support. She had prospered on Wall Street, but she was a child of the working people who had not forgotten her own origins. In the clash between workers and bosses, she threw her weight on the side of those who labored. Meanwhile, the *Weekly* had been taking on a more strident tone, uncovering corruption in the real-estate schemes of railroad and insurance companies. The *Weekly* was a brave early voice in a journalistic tradition that would become known as "muckraking."

With her newspaper broadcasting her anticapitalist sympathies, Woodhull announced her intentions to mount a broad-based reform campaign. She arranged her own nomination to the Presidency by a citizens' group called the Victoria League, a group she apparently called into being herself. Allowing some uncertainty to hover about the origins of the league, Woodhull answered its call to lead a newly-formed Equal Rights Party to demand suffrage from Congress. "The right woman," she wrote to the Victoria League, who "struck the right chord of the public sympathy and confidence" could "ride triumphantly on the tide of a joyous popular tumult to the supreme political position." But it was not suffrage alone that she would seek. She wrote to the Victoria League that "the freedom of women and the freedom of the laborer are conjointly the cause of humanity."

er
ong
e
n

he
that
be
re
ntry.

Those who believed that Victoria Woodhull was mostly a spokesperson for Stephen Pearl Andrews noticed the inconsistency in her position. On Wall Street her brokerage speculated in gold, while at the Cooper Institute the candidate recommended a national currency that would devalue gold. The contradiction seemed not to have troubled Woodhull. Like Anthony, who had said she would take money from the devil himself in the cause of woman suffrage, Woodhull played the stock markets of high finance to win the profits that allowed her reform campaign to continue. Although the press had loved the Wall Street broker, they were growing less tolerant of the Cooper Institute labor leader. Woodhull was speaking at a time when scenes of the bloody uprisings of the Paris Commune were still fresh ink for the American newspaper-reading public. For a few months that year, France had been governed by a revolutionary group called the Communards, whose brief control was celebrated by international socialist leader Karl Marx as the first victory of the working classes against their capitalist oppressors. Although Woodhull marched down the streets of New York later that December in a procession that honored the fallen heroes of the Commune, she was not seeking a violent overthrow of capitalist power.

In the spring and summer of 1871, Wood
speeches at New York City's Cooper Institute
allied herself with the National Labor Union,
first national federation of unions. In "The
Problems of Labor and Capital," Woodhull dec
reforms the labor union movement sought
rights. Addressing the land-grabbing schemes c
millionaires, Woodhull announced that "th
which we stand is as common property as the
we are surrounded."

Indeed, to many it seemed that the develo
railroads had been made possible only by feder
enriched families such as the Rockefellers, the
and the Astors at the great expense of ordii
During President Lincoln's administration, the
Act of 1862 had promised 160 acres of western
an acre to anyone who would cultivate the land
Because few working people could lay hands on
$200, the land frequently fell into the hands c
who possessed the ready cash. Meanwhile, mc
million acres of land were given as outright gif
railroad companies by Congress and the President
panies would hold the land until it increased in va
it at enormous profits. Two million five hundr
families might have been given house and land i
ceded to the railroads had been given over to
Woodhull argued in one of her Cooper Institute a

Woodhull's political platform advocated
ownership of the nation's railroads, an end to h
imported goods that enabled domestic manu
raise prices, and the establishment of a nationa
rency of "greenbacks" to replace the fluctuati
private bank notes backed up by the gold reser
known as the gold standard). Increasing the ci
the cheaper paper money would put more ca
pockets of working people.

*The "Greenback
Movement," ofter
promoted in news-
papers, emerged a
the Civil War an
those opposed to t
government's retu
to gold currency.
Woodhull joined
movement, urging
a national currenc
based on the "ent
wealth" of the cou*

EQUALITY, NOT JUST FREEDOM

Victoria Woodhull's speech "On the Impending Revolution," delivered in Boston and New York in February 1872, so alarmed conservative society that the mainstream press, fearful that she was inciting riot, launched a campaign against her. Among those who felt her barbs were directed against them was most probably her patron Cornelius Vanderbilt. In the speech, Woodhull claimed that her call for land and finance reforms lay in her interpretation of the Christian Bible, not in the communism of Karl Marx.

Since those who possess the accumulated wealth of the country have filched it by legal means from those to whom it justly belongs—the people—it must be returned to them, by legal means if possible, but it must be returned to them in any event. When a person worth millions dies, instead of leaving it to his children, who have no more title to it than anybody else's children have, it must revert to the people, who really produced it. Do you say that is injustice to the children? I say, No! And if you ask me how the rich man's children are going to live after his death, I answer, by the same means as the poor man's children live. Let it be remembered that we have had simple freedom quite long enough. By setting all our hopes on freedom we have been robbed of our rights. What we want now is more than freedom—we want equality! And by the Heaven above us, earth's growing children are going to have it! What right have the children of the rich to be born to luxurious idleness . . . ? Do [the children of the rich and poor] not in common belong to God's human family? If I mistake not, Christ told us so. You will not dispute his authority, I am sure. If instead of preaching Christ and him crucified quite so much, we should practice his teaching a little more, my word for it, we should all be better Christians. If, in getting [their rights], the people find bayonets opposing them, it will be not be their fault if they make their way through them by the aid of bayonets.

Woodhull's call for reform was based on a belief in the legitimacy of the people's rights, which they might win with the ballot. Even her earlier declaration to the women's convention that "we mean revolution, we mean secession," had been made as a rallying cry to storm the polling places with ballots in hand rather than as a military call to arms. "Political power consists in a majority of votes cast," she reminded her audience at the Cooper Institute in the summer of 1871. "Of what have the male laboring class to complain?" she asked. "They outnumber and can consequently outvote the capitalist class."

But reforms had to be made. "The extreme of individual wealth and poverty is in direct antagonism to a democratic government," she told her audience. She had seen the rat-infested garbage lying in the streets of the poor neighborhoods of the city, while ostentatious mansions in the manner of European palaces were being raised on Fifth Avenue. If in one of those mansions her old friend and financial backer Commodore Vanderbilt was wondering about Woodhull's eagerness to separate him from his profits, he was for the moment silent.

When the time came to put into practice the militancy of the "New Departure" strategy for woman suffrage, Woodhull marched a group of women to a polling place on a city-wide regional election day. While the polling inspectors shrugged helplessly, she raised her fist in a defiant gesture, claiming that the 14th and 15th Amendments had enfranchised her. Her ballot and those of the women who followed her to the polls were rejected. Still, a newspaper drawing caught the confident authority of her posture, the posture of a woman who could command impressive lecturing fees and receive respectful notice from the press.

In the fall of 1871, Woodhull traveled to Vineland, New Jersey, and to Troy, New York, to seek the support of the spiritualists for her Presidential campaign. The spiritualists were impressed by Woodhull's belief in human rights and progress, which meshed with their own thinking. When she claimed that she received oracular visions from the ancient Greek orator Demosthenes, she secured her standing among them. "I have been a spiritualist and a recipient of heavenly favors ever since I can remember," she told them. Indeed, it is likely that she could not explain in any other words the mystical sensibility she recalled in herself from childhood. No group of supporters seemed to belong to her as naturally as the groups that gathered in Vineland and Troy.

Nor did adding the spiritualists to the labor and suffragist camps make for an unlikely grouping. Though only some suffragists were enthusiastic spiritualists, virtually all spiritualists believed in reforms, particularly women's rights reform. They had sought temperance laws banning alcohol to save women from abuse by drunken male relatives. They favored vegetarianism, believing that killing animals was a form of male violence. They were natural opponents of authority figures, whether these were church leaders, unsympathetic legislators, industrial and financial tycoons, or paternal heads of families. The spiritualists were so

Victoria Woodhull attends an 1873 spiritualist camp meeting in Plympton, Massachusetts; her second husband, Colonel Blood is seated at her left. Between Blood and Woodhull sits an admirer, the free-thinking future publisher Benjamin Tucker.

unused to organizational formalities that they rather surprised themselves in endorsing Woodhull, even electing her president of the American Association of Spiritualists. Several outspoken veterans of the movement contested the election. One complained that Woodhull's spiritualism ran second to her political ambitions, echoing the suspicions of Susan B. Anthony, who was beginning to doubt that woman suffrage was primary in Woodhull's mind.

Anthony's suspicions were heightened in January 1872, when Woodhull traveled to Washington, D.C., for another National Woman Suffrage Convention. Woodhull's position among these eminent women was very different from what it had been a year earlier. Now she was the Presidential nominee of an emerging Equal Rights Party and the leader of the American Association of Spiritualists. Moreover, she trailed an impressive record of public lectures on issues of finance and economics about which no other woman had ever spoken so lucidly. If her lecture on social freedoms had made her notorious in some circles, it had won her respect in others.

In one matter, however, Woodhull came to the woman suffrage meeting less well-equipped. With her brokerage failing, she was in straitened financial circumstances. The $10,000 donation she had promised to the suffrage movement a year earlier may never have been paid, although she incurred expenses printing out the call for the meeting and helping with its organization. Planning her own favorable reception at the convention, Woodhull adroitly recommended to Isabella Beecher Hooker that there should be some spiritualists among the men who deserved invitations to the convention.

In fact, Woodhull succeeded at this Washington convention far more dramatically than she may have anticipated. Given a prominent place on the first evening's agenda, she reminded her audience of her Memorial a year earlier, scoffing at the logic of the House Judiciary Committee that had rejected it. Woodhull argued that it was useless to look for help from the Republicans or Democrats. She did not, she insisted, propose to wait "sixty years for justice." "I want it here and now," she affirmed, not only for women, but for the men and women "who toil all their lives only to see the results of their labor poured . . . into the coffers of the already rich." "What I shall now propose means revolution" she ended, "the voice of the people heard as the government of this country."

Susan B. Anthony had argued in 1868, when she had briefly won support for suffrage from the women's typesetter union, that the problems of working-class women would best be solved by giving women the vote. She heard in Woodhull's denunciation of Republicans and Democrats a not-so-veiled plea for support for Woodhull's new Equal Rights Party with herself at the helm. The next morning Anthony told the convention "Any party that is a woman suffrage party I am for, and I will help to fly its kite, but I am not willing to be the last little paper knot in the tail of any political kite."

In spite of Anthony, the convention closed with an endorsement of Woodhull, resolving that "We rejoice in the rapidly organizing millions of spiritualists, labor reformers, temperance and educational forces now simultaneously waking to their need of woman's help in the cause of reform." After Stephen Pearl Andrews, at the head of a group of labor reformers, had applauded the Equal Rights Party, a wave of support for Woodhull swept through the convention. Suffragist and spiritualist Ada Ballou ran from the stage to the rear of the auditorium so that her proposal that the Convention endorse Woodhull's Presidential candidacy would appear to come from the floor. Despite Anthony's impromptu speech in opposition, the proposal carried. Victoria Woodhull left the Washington convention as its acclaimed candidate.

The coalition Woodhull had formed to support the Equal Rights Party was fragile at best. But weeks later, in a stirring address in New York City entitled "The Impending

Revolution," Woodhull appealed to all her supporters—suffragists, spiritualists, and labor reformers—whose needs for equality and justice, she argued, were first defended in the teachings of Jesus Christ. In February 1872, Woodhull stood before a crowded audience at the Academy of Music on 14th Street in a black jacket and a tie, her curly hair floating freely over her shoulders, her arms raised dramatically. The audience was prepared to be astounded by the "terrible Victoria Woodhull," as the newspapers called her. By now her platform was familiar: return land to the people, end the gold standard, nationalize the railroads, end taxes on imported goods. To these familiar reforms she added a call for free public education for boys and girls in the arts and sciences, and in "a practical knowledge of some productive branch of labor."

Woodhull had become more militant than she had been months earlier when she first wooed labor reformers. She was willing now to name those millionaires whose great wealth depended on the labor of the poor, including Commodore Vanderbilt. "A Vanderbilt may sit in his office and manipulate stocks, or make dividends, by which, in a few years, he amasses fifty million dollars from the industries of the country, and he is one of the remarkable men of the age. But if a poor, half-starved child were to take a loaf of bread from his cupboard to prevent starvation, she would be sent to the Tombs," she protested, naming the infamous prison in Manhattan. "What right have the children of the rich to be born to luxurious idleness?" she asked.

As a clairvoyant, Woodhull claimed to have foreseen the Civil War, and now once again she could hear "the rattle of musketry, and the roar of cannon," as a more terrible contest approached. She appealed to her audience to avoid the bloody strife she foresaw by joining a human rights party that would unite the various partisans—temperance advocates, labor reformers, spiritualists, suffragists. She did not name her own Equal Rights Party, but there could be no doubt where such a party was to be found.

Until now the press had treated Woodhull with patronizing mockery or grudging respect. But as she began declaring that some of New York's most powerful men were thieves who stole money from ordinary people, the *New York Times* raised the alarm. Woodhull's loosely defined socialism seemed to invoke the ideas of Karl Marx, who claimed that the violent overthrow of the capitalist class was inevitable, if not imminent. In spite of her professed confidence in the power of the ballot, Woodhull's speech sounded like the anthem of revolution.

The *New York Times* suggested that Woodhull "prove her faith in the theory that property is crime" and divest herself of "black silk, her jaunty sealskin jacket, her diamond rings." When the *Times* refused to print her reply, she published her letter in the *Weekly*. "I never objected to the accumulation of wealth," she protested, adding she demanded only that equal conditions should prevail and that the rights of working people should be respected.

The blend of democracy and spiritualism that Woodhull espoused was not in fact Marxist socialism. She was the first American publisher to print Marx's *Communist Manifesto* (in her *Weekly*), and in 1871 she had taken over the leadership of a New York woman's section (Section 12) of Marx's International Workingmen's Association. But Karl Marx's London office was quite justifiably skeptical of Woodhull's politics, and called her a "pseudo communist." Unlike Marx, Woodhull had no quarrel with the private ownership of property, and she regarded Section 12 as another group she might enlist in support of her campaign. Towards those ends, she gave space in the *Weekly* to Section 12 meeting announcements and expositions on communism. In December 1871, she had marched in a procession to honor the fallen heroes of the Commune. But the communism she, along with many other spiritualists who were members of Section 12, professed resembled a biblical workers' paradise with wealth shared more fairly and human rights universally possessed, rather than Marx's vision of a working class taking over the ownership of the factories.

Still, the militancy with which she now demanded labor reforms had been noticed. "She is . . . capable of mischief in inflaming the unthinking hostility of the poor to the rich," complained the *New York Times*. If Woodhull intended to shake the citadels of capitalism, perhaps it was time to undermine her worrisome influence. Not long after she delivered "The Impending Revolution," the illustrator Thomas Nast damned her in caricature as a "Mrs. Satan" who preached free love. The illustration was widely published, and Woodhull's reputation suffered.

Another blow was struck by Susan B. Anthony, who in the spring of 1872 at last broke ranks with Woodhull. Anthony had admired the brains, the cash, and the cool confidence of the woman whose measure she had taken in Washington more than a year earlier. But the cash was not forthcoming, and the confident intelligence now struck Anthony as being employed less in the service of woman suffrage than in the service of Woodhull's own career. Moreover, Anthony had watched as the New York suffragist wing's connection with Woodhull alienated supporters, who drifted into their own separate associations. Now Woodhull was planning a political meeting in May at Apollo Hall, where she hoped that both the suffragists and the labor union movement would join her. At their own meeting, however, the National Labor Union nominated another candidate for the Presidency. The woman suffrage convention, meeting in New York in May as it had for decades, was scheduled for Steinway Hall a day before Woodhull's party was to meet in Apollo Hall.

Before their convention opened, the two old friends Stanton and Anthony argued for hours about whether to support Woodhull. The more radical Stanton found much in Woodhull that echoed her own convictions, but the strategist Anthony would not tie suffrage, as she had earlier said, to anyone else's political kite. Despite Anthony's opposition, Woodhull spoke early in the convention's meeting. Woodhull urged the suffragists to support the economic reforms working-class women sought. In a startling bid for power, she invited the suffragists to adjourn their meeting and join hers at Apollo Hall the next day.

But Susan B. Anthony had no intention of ending her own meeting to support the candidacy of Victoria Woodhull. Refusing to call the vote to adjourn that Woodhull demanded, Anthony ruled her out of order. In a dramatic confrontation between the two women, Victoria Woodhull clung to the podium and continued speaking, while Anthony left the stage and directed the janitor of Steinway Hall to shut off all the lights. In the sudden darkness, the suffragists vacated the meeting.

The next day, whatever their private regrets, Isabella Beecher Hooker and Stanton remained loyal to Anthony. The suffragists met again in the re-illuminated Steinway while Woodhull moved to Apollo Hall. There, among spiritualists and representatives of Section 12 of the International Workingmen's Association, Woodhull found sympathy, fervor, and concord. Under a pseudonym that may have been Isabella Beecher Hooker's, one witness wrote for the *Weekly:* "As I approached the place, I heard the voice of Mrs. Woodhull resounding through the hall . . . She stood there, dressed in plain black, with flushed face, gleaming eye, locks partly disheveled, upraised arm and quivering under the fire of her own rhapsody. She seemed at moments like one possessed, and the eloquence which poured from her lips in reckless torrents swept through the souls of the multitude." With deafening shouts of approval, the multitudes at Apollo Hall nominated Woodhull for the Presidency. An hour or so of debate over a Vice President finally yielded the name of Frederick Douglass, although the great abolitionist was not present at Apollo Hall and had not volunteered to run.

The Equal Rights Party proposed a political platform that incorporated all of the reforms that Woodhull had been urging during the previous year: the call for woman suffrage that had begun her work; demands for labor reform that would become part of the American labor union movement; and planks for land and railroad reform that would be taken up by the American Populist Party, a political reform movement that spread through midwestern and southern politics from the 1870s to the 1890s. Although she could not claim to be, as she had hoped, the leader of the suffrage and labor movements, Victoria Woodhull had gathered a youthful, vibrant, and hybrid constituency, idealistic and individualistic by nature. For the nearly 700 people at Apollo Hall, representing 22 states and 4 territories, she was, for the moment, their standard-bearer.

Back in the suffrage camp two days later, Isabella Beecher Hooker took time to write a long, newsy letter to her friend "Lizzie" Stanton. Although she would not desert Anthony, she had followed the events at Apollo Hall closely. "Apollo Hall was a success," she crowed. Hooker foresaw a strengthened suffrage army, moving now on several fronts. To be sure, she confessed, "Victoria has been a heavy load." But "she has been and still is the one instrument for working out the deliverance from bondage and she has opened

Victoria Woodhull is nominated for the Presidency of the United States at a meeting of the Equal Rights Party in New York City on May 10, 1872. Woodhull proclaimed dramatically, "From this convention will go forth a tide of revolution that shall sweep over the whole world."

the Red Sea before us who were willing to pass through under her leadership."

For the moment, Hooker was not worried about the radical economic platform of the Apollo Hall meeting, where she had seen red flags and revolutionary slogans mounted on the walls. She wrote to Stanton that she believed the labor reform community would work for woman suffrage because they would want "the prestige of our social position." As for the suffragists, "we want the vague shadowy horror that haunts politicians the moment that bloody revolution is threatened by the ignorant—though often good hearted leaders of the oppressed working classes . . . We are the link between the extremes of respectability and mobocracy," she told Stanton, who can "guide the advancing hosts." As for the suffragists who were disparaging Woodhull, she wished they would "show us where the money and brains and unceasing energy . . . would have come from if she had not been moved to present her Memorial and follow it up with the prodigious outlays of the last year and a half."

Isabella Beecher Hooker could not have known that Woodhull's pockets were emptying. She did read, however, that in the spring Canning Woodhull had at last succumbed to the disease of alcoholism that had racked his body for years. A quiet presence in the Woodhull household, he had taken on, while he could, some of the care of his afflicted son Byron. Had Victoria Woodhull not given him a home, Canning would have died on the streets.

Woodhull's tribute to her first husband in the *Weekly* raised not a word of blame. Whatever wretched memories of neglect and privation lingered from those early years, she put them behind her to present a proud face to the world. As she sought political influence and advancement, she presented Canning Woodhull to the world as an admirable gentleman. With more respectable connections, Victoria Woodhull knew, she might seem less dangerous to the public whose opinions she sought to shape.

The Beecher-Tilton trial, in a time before newsreels, was reported in illustrated "verbatim reports" giving a blow-by-blow description of the entire proceedings. The aggrieved husband Theodore Tilton (top row, second from left) stares fixedly across businessman Francis Moulton to the portrait of Henry Ward Beecher, whom Tilton accused of adultery with his wife. At opposite ends of the bottom row are Tilton's diminutive wife Libby (left) and Beecher's accuser Victoria Woodhull. Trial judge Chief Justice Joseph Neilson, surrounded by portraits of witnesses, accusers, and defenders, represents the justice system itself with the centrality of an impartial observer.

6

STANDING ALONE: WOODHULL UNDER ATTACK

My friends and fellow citizens I come into your presence from the American Bastille to which I was consigned by the cowardly servility of the age.

—Victoria Woodhull, speech at Cooper Institute, January 1873

Troubles lay ahead. Woodhull needed money now to pay the legal expenses and filing fees required to put her name on state ballots for the Presidential election coming up in November 1872. She was drawing good money in lecture fees, but traveling from city to city took its toll on her stamina, and regretfully she postponed a trek west that would have brought in welcome revenues. Tennie was ready to help out, and made her debut as a lecturer in New York City offering "Behind the Scenes in Wall Street," but still the house on 38th Street was far too expensive to maintain.

Woodhull moved her family to rooms near Apollo Hall temporarily, she hoped, until financial backers of her political campaign would relieve their difficulties. Far from such relief, however, Woodhull was beset with disappointments. Frederick Douglass declined the Vice-Presidential place on the ticket with her. Susan B. Anthony wrote to Isabella

Beecher Hooker that undoubtedly Douglass didn't think the nomination important enough to notice. Another blow was struck when Section 12 of the International Workingmen's Association was expelled from the Association by the London office, which cited an insufficient number of working-class members enrolled.

Meanwhile, Horace Greeley, *New York Tribune* editor and foe of woman suffrage, had become the candidate of a coalition of liberal Republicans and Democrats, drawing the backing of Woodhull's former admirer Theodore Tilton, who may have hoped for employment from Greeley. Whatever hopes Woodhull may have harbored for the support of the liberal wing of the suffrage movement were short lived. When the Republican Party of Ulysses S. Grant included in its platform a promise to consider women's suffrage, Susan B. Anthony pledged her support, taking with her Elizabeth Cady Stanton, even though Stanton called the plank a mere "splinter."

More immediately ominous, Commodore Vanderbilt abandoned his protégée. His desertion was no surprise, for Woodhull was now widely accused of having taken up communist sympathies. Indeed, with a national strike for an eight-hour workday threatened for May, many businessmen were ready to lash out against the labor movement and its supporters. Without Vanderbilt's support, the brokerage foundered, soon to go under during the "black seventies," as the imminent economic depression was to be called. Woodhull later wrote that she suspected a conspiracy was forming against her. "Those with whom we transacted business were sought out," she said, "their minds poisoned against us, and to our own astonishment one by one they fell away until we stood alone."

Even more harmful to the campaign, Woodhull felt compelled to suspend publication of the *Weekly* temporarily because the journal was losing some of its financial sponsors. Without her newspaper, Woodhull lost direct access to supporters to whom she would have appealed for help. The loss was great. Woodhull was justifiably proud of the *Weekly*, which she called "a free and independent paper—not afraid to deal with all subjects in plain terms."

Meanwhile, Woodhull was finding doors closing to her as she searched for lodgings for a family that still included her 12-year-old daughter Zulu and her helpless son Byron. Having taken shelter at the Gilsey House, one of the new hotels on 29th Street near Fifth Avenue, Woodhull was appalled when the hotel proprietor asked her to find other accommodations. She had grown so notorious, he explained, that his family boarders would leave rather than remain under the same roof with her. Stung, Woodhull demanded to know why she deserved such an insult. The proprietor reminded her that she had advocated free love.

In her great need, Woodhull sought out the help of Henry Ward Beecher, the Brooklyn minister who had failed to stand beside her at Steinway Hall when she had challenged him to acknowledge his belief in free love. "Now I want your assistance," she wrote to Beecher, asking him to intervene to help her stay on at the hotel. The *Herald* later reported that Beecher called it a "whining" letter and declined to help.

One night when she returned from her office, Woodhull found her hotel rooms at the Gilsey House locked against her, and her belongings left outside. "Sick and weary," she recalled later, "we vainly sought for other lodgings. No hotel would receive us, and finally, at one o'clock at night, we were obliged to return to our office in Broad Street and sleep as best we could upon the floor." Dispirited, Woodhull and her family lived for weeks in this way until one of her sisters found them a house.

It seemed incongruous to Woodhull that so many thousands of people crowded eagerly into her lecture halls or wrote her deploring the absence of the *Weekly*, while landlords in the same city refused her board. "Everyone seemed to be possessed of the general sentiment of bitterness that prevailed at the time," she wrote later. Later, when funds from friends enabled her to restore publication of the *Weekly*, she described her mood of baffled gloom. She traveled in September to a Boston meeting of the American Association of Spiritualists and declared herself to be "tired, sick, and discouraged," ready to abandon her most faithful constituency, the spiritualists, and ready to decline their renomination as their president. Instead she was revitalized as she encountered new accusations being spread against her.

This time Susan B. Anthony was responsible, suggesting that Woodhull was blackmailing women suffrage leaders who were speaking out against her. Earlier that spring Woodhull had indeed sent out drafts of an article to various prominent suffragists that threatened to expose their own secret sexual relations outside of marriage. Some rumors claimed that Woodhull demanded money in return for silence. Publishing a defense of herself in the *Weekly*, Woodhull insisted that she only wished to end their campaign of abuse against her. As for Anthony, she may have lent her prestigious name to the accusation in hopes of damaging Woodhull's standing among some suffragists.

As Buck Claflin's daughter, Woodhull was no stranger to the practice of blackmail. The feuding Claflins often threatened each other with exposure of crimes real or imagined. An editorial in the *Weekly* had even defended blackmail as the practice of powerless women against abusive rich and influential men, particularly when the woman's intention was to expose hypocrisy rather than to extract money. Woodhull denied vehemently in the *Weekly* that she would ever have taken money from Henry Ward Beecher to buy her silence. Still, the blackmail charge, surfacing again and again, stuck to Woodhull and embarrassed her. Angrily she remembered that she had pressed Beecher to stand beside her at Steinway Hall, threatening him with exposure. But in the end she had not revealed him to that audience as a free

As many as 3,000 listeners might assemble in Henry Ward Beecher's Plymouth Church in Brooklyn, New York, to hear the popular minister deliver sermons so overflowing in sentiment that critics called his ministry the "religion of gush."

lover. Beecher remained in his ministry at Plymouth Church even though it was so widely whispered that he preached the sacredness of his marriage vows every Sunday to pews filled with his former and current mistresses.

As Victoria Woodhull rose to address the convention of spiritualists in Boston in September 1872, Henry Ward Beecher's hypocrisy was not far from her mind. The fact that his reputation remained inviolate while slanderers heaped insults upon hers was galling. She recounted in the *Weekly* that she was suddenly seized with "an overwhelming gust of inspiration" and, as if in a trance, revealed to the assembly the story of Beecher's secret love affair with Elizabeth Tilton, the wife of Theodore Tilton. This was old gossip that had been whispered about ever since Woodhull had first been introduced into the socially prominent suffragist circle at the Washington convention three years earlier. But while even the venerable Paulina Wright Davis had encouraged her to expose the "mass of Beecher corruption," she had never before named Henry Ward Beecher publicly.

Woodhull left Boston having been reelected president of the American Association of Spiritualists, while the story of the Beecher affair traveled by word of mouth. Although

115

the principals of the story were eminently newsworthy, the Boston press maintained a discreet silence about Beecher, as did most of the major newspapers in New York. Still, the tumult had shaken Woodhull free from her doldrums, and she left on a long-delayed lecture tour on which packed houses clamored to hear her, her notoriety having only increased her popularity.

When Woodhull returned to New York, she resumed her attack on Beecher and on all of the respectable New Yorkers whom she believed were leagued against her, those who had been willing to let her roam the streets without a hotel to give her room. With an infusion of revenue from the successful lecture tour, she resurrected the *Weekly* and put out a special issue highlighting her revelations about Henry Ward Beecher. The first run of 100,000 copies completely sold out. Some of the buyers were Beecher supporters, who purchased and destroyed copies as soon as they reached the stands.

There were many reasons why Beecher's associates wished to silence Woodhull. The charismatic and widely respected Beecher was at the hub of a network of newspaper and book publishing interests that profited from his popularity and would suffer losses from any harm to his reputation. Commenting on the emerging scandal, Elizabeth Cady Stanton noted caustically in a letter to the *Chicago Tribune* that "The church property is not taxed, its bonds in the hands of wealthy men of that organization are valuable, and the bondholders, alive to their financial interests, stand around Mr. Beecher, a faithful, protecting band, not loving truth and justice less, but their own pockets more."

If Beecher were exposed as an adulterer, the readership of his newspaper, the *Christian Union,* might fall away, and his volume of the *Life of Christ,* newly in print, would sell less well, as would his book of sermons. The ferries that carried passengers each Sunday from Manhattan to Brooklyn's Plymouth Church would be far less busy.

Beecher's popularity, which profited so many commercial interests, also lay in important alterations in America's cultural and religious attitudes. In his sermons, Beecher tempered the stern Protestantism of an earlier generation with a more passionate expression of religious feeling. He called for a more emotional response to religion, believing that such a response would also correct what he saw as an increasing sterility in American national life. To a man like Beecher, the expansion of cities and the growth of commerce and industry had severed the natural bond between Americans and land, sapping their natural vitality. Privately, Beecher believed that passionate friendships between men and women who were not married to each other were appropriate and even important. Woodhull claimed in the *Weekly* that Beecher told her that marriage was the "grave of happiness." But Beecher would not have said so much from the pulpit at Plymouth Church. Instead, as the Herald reported, he proclaimed "I stand on the New England doctrine in which I was brought up, that it is best for a man to have one wife, and that he stay by her and that he not meddle with his neighbors' wives."

Beecher's rush to confirm a traditional belief in marriage reflected an alteration in public moral sentiment in post–Civil War America. Some of the experimental tolerance that characterized the years after the Civil War was now giving way to a social conservatism. In the South, the period of political realignment and black enfranchisement called Reconstruction had come to an end. The Ku Klux Klan and a militant racism were enforcing traditional white authority and undoing gains won after the war. The same retrenchment was weakening possibilities for social reform. Voices protested that looser divorce laws were weakening the family, which was understood to be the foundation stone of a stable society. Even Isabella Beecher Hooker, who remained loyal to Woodhull as the Beecher scandal widened, worried that Woodhull was giving too much authority to men to wander from their marriage vows. Should such a respectable marriage as Henry Ward Beecher's become raked with scandal, marriage could hardly be the bedrock it claimed to be. Woodhull was exposing more than just Beecher. By calling Beecher a "poltroon, a coward, and a sneak," in her special edition of the *Weekly,* Woodhull was lifting the veil on the imperfect state of middle-class marriage itself.

Beecher sat out the assault in dignified silence and refused to sue Woodhull for libel. But in November 1872 another outraged reader of the *Weekly* rose to do battle. Anthony Comstock was a vigilante crusading against sin and obscenity. The Founder of the New York Society for the Suppression of Vice, he had successfully lobbied Congress in June 1872 to strengthen existing laws prohibiting sending obscene publications through the U.S. mail. Widely disliked as a smug zealot, Comstock believed that God had sent him to sinful New York, which he described as "at the mouth of a sewer in the middle of a swamp."

Ignoring the widespread traffic of pornography rampant elsewhere in the city, Comstock seized upon the *Weekly* both for its story of the Beecher-Tilton scandal and for a few fateful lines in a separate piece that Tennie had written. Calling attention to the double standard that permitted so much freedom to men but not to women, Tennie had quoted some lurid bragging by a prominent New York broker named Luther Challis, in which he described his seduction of a young girl. Having arranged to have a copy of this edition of the *Weekly* mailed to him, Comstock brought charges against Woodhull and Claflin on grounds of sending obscenity through the U.S. mail. Luther Challis denied the stories printed about him in the Weekly and sued Woodhull and Claflin for libel.

When the *Weekly* identified Luther Challis as a client of houses of prostitution, Woodhull and Claflin's threats to expose the influential patrons of New York's many brothels seemed on the verge of being carried out. Some who might have supported the *Weekly's* right to free speech were worried into silence. The sisters would be the first victims of Congress's newly strengthened "Comstock" laws, instruments of repression that waged war on social reformers, free thinkers, and disseminators of birth control and abortion information until well into the twentieth century.

Meanwhile, Woodhull's own painful odyssey through the court system began. On Saturday, November 2, 1872, Woodhull and Tennie returned to their Broad Street office to find U.S. deputy marshals waiting to take them into custody. Following the story with avid interest, the *Herald* reported that crowds gathered to dog the footsteps of the "notorious female brokers" up the rickety stairs of the police court at Jefferson Market. The *Herald* described Woodhull as "grave and severe," listening with "painful interest" to the *Weekly* being described as "vulgar, indecent, and obscene." Remanded into custody, the sisters were sent to the Ludlow Street Jail, where, the *Herald* reported, their all-male fellow prisoners agreed to stop smoking, "in honor of the female visitors."

As Woodhull steps down from her carriage ahead of her sister Tennessee, a policeman presents her with a warrant for her arrest. She blamed the obscenity charges on retaliation by Beecher supporters.

Woodhull and Tennie remained in jail for four weeks. Election day passed them by, giving Ulysses S. Grant another term in office. As Comstock widened his net to harass Colonel Blood with arrest, some sympathy for Woodhull grew. In the next four weeks, the sisters were released, arrested again, re-released, and re-arrested. Friends mounted bail again and again for a succession of charges leveled.

In the new year 1873, after her friends had been able to post bail on her behalf, Woodhull once again took to the lecture circuit. Now, months after her first arrest, she was both more wary and more defiant. Harriet Beecher Stowe had used her influence to prevent Woodhull from speaking in Boston, where she was denied a license to appear at the Music Hall. As she prepared next to speak at New York's Cooper Institute, Woodhull learned that the police lay waiting to arrest her again. Dressed in the costume of an old and feeble Quaker woman, Woodhull passed unnoticed into the lecture hall and made her way slowly to the stage, where the young spiritualist speaker Laura Cuppy Smith was promising the audience that Woodhull would appear.

"Yes, I am here," Woodhull announced, dashing from behind a pillar, old age, coal-scuttle bonnet, and gray dress disappearing like magic, the *Times* reported. One spectator described the scene: "There stood Victoria C. Woodhull, an overwhelming inspirational fire scintillating from her eyes and beaming from her face . . . her arms raised aloft in nervous excitement, her hair in wild and graceful confusion, and her head thrown back defiantly . . . she looked the personification of Liberty in Arms."

"My friends and fellow citizens," Woodhull told the crowd, "I come into your presence from a cell in the American Bastille to which I was consigned by the cowardly servility of the age." For an hour and a half Woodhull held her audience's rapt attention. She was now, she believed, a martyr for the social revolution she was advocating. Just a few days earlier she had written a cordial letter to

Susan B. Anthony, who was herself facing court proceedings for thrusting her ballot at a cowed polling inspector on election day and voting illegally for President Grant. "There is no time now to indulge in personal enmity," wrote Woodhull. "I fear they intend to crush out in your person the constitutional question of women's suffrage, as they are attempting in my person to establish a precedent for the suppression of recalcitrant journals." Anthony did not reply to Woodhull's letter.

That January night at the Cooper Institute, Woodhull defended the idea of free love from the charge that such a doctrine meant that promiscuity would run riot. "Free love means nothing more and nothing less, in kind, than free worship, freedom of the press, freedom of conscience, free trade, free thought." Her social revolution, she implied, was simply the next stage in the American Revolution, the extension of certain inalienable rights belonging to all citizens, a revolution whose grass roots lay in American experimental communities and in the socialism of the New Testament, not of the Paris Commune. When she ended her lecture, she calmly gave herself up to the waiting marshals, who took her off to the Ludlow Street jail. As the marshals moved forward, the auditorium filled with howls of protest.

Woodhull, her sister, and Colonel Blood would again be arrested, released on bail, and re-arrested in the days to follow, on such uncertain charges of libel and obscenity that the arresting officers were sometimes unable to name the precise complaint. The criminal lawyer William F. Howe argued on Woodhull's behalf that the obscenity laws of 1872, promoted by Comstock, had not specifically included newspapers in those materials enjoined from sending pornography through the mails. Sensing an attack on their free speech, some newspapers at last spoke up for Woodhull. At the Ludlow Street jail, bail charges for Woodhull were greater even than those leveled against the infamous Boss William Tweed, who was finally arrested after draining millions of dollars from the city's treasury. Although it seemed increasingly evident that the obscenity charge could not stand, the judge still held the matter over for a jury decision.

The persecution of Woodhull grew even meaner. One of the arrests during the days following the Cooper Institute speech was delayed until late in the day to prevent Woodhull and Tennie from making bail before the close of business. Rather than sending her to her usual cell in the fairly new Ludlow Street jail, the sheriff escorted the sisters to the Tombs, a massive granite prison built 35 years earlier in the style of an Egyptian mausoleum. Standing on damp ground and housing twice as many inmates as there was room for, the Tombs made for grim quarters. Its walls were encrusted in mold and the cells filthy and vermin-infested. Incarceration in the Tombs could break any prisoner's spirit.

Some of Woodhull's friends were cowed into silence, most notably the suffragists who met later in May for their annual convention with only the faithful Isabella Beecher Hooker daring to mention Woodhull's name. Elizabeth Cady Stanton thought it wise to distance herself from the woman whose courage on social issues she admired, although she knew, as did Susan B. Anthony and Paulina Wright Davis, that Woodhull's revelations about Henry Ward Beecher were widely believed. Indeed, the story had first been confided to Anthony by Elizabeth Tilton herself. As for Davis, who had encouraged Woodhull to reveal the "Beecher corruption," she was ill in Europe, and, although she hoped to return to help defend Woodhull, she asked that her name not be made public. Her hesitation was well founded. Isabella Hooker, whose name was dragged into the papers as a confederate of Woodhull's, was threatened with commitment to a mental asylum for deserting her Beecher kin, a fate not unusual for rebellious women of good families.

For the time, the spiritualist community remained loyal. Most helpfully, Benjamin Butler, the congressman who had been Woodhull's supporter when she delivered the Memorial to the House Judiciary Committee in 1871, wrote a public letter to the *New York Sun* supporting the defense lawyer's claim that the obscenity charge was illegal. Fortunately, the resurrected *Weekly,* Woodhull's most important means of disseminating her defense, was selling widely. When the New York newspapers served up Catharine Beecher's new accusation of blackmail against Woodhull, not one other newspaper was willing to print Woodhull's denial of the charge.

Meanwhile, the pattern of arrest and imprisonment, release on bail, and re-arrest was undermining Woodhull's health. With her financial resources drained to make bail, Woodhull's public lecturing became her family's sole source of income besides the *Weekly*. To meet the exhausting demands of travel, with its overheated railroad cars and freezing stations, Woodhull relied on her stage presence— her voice, magnetism, and stamina. Only she could "run the machine," as Colonel Blood put it. But she was running on a reserve of energy that was becoming depleted.

It was raining on one warm evening in June when she returned home from the weary rounds of currying favor with newspaper offices for column space to make her arguments. She wondered, not unreasonably, if her next home was to be the federal prison "up the river" at Sing Sing, in Ossining, New York. She was ill, she told Tennie, who brought her tea. As Colonel Blood helped her upstairs she collapsed. Tennie called doctors in to help, not sure whether her sister was still living. For several days, as Woodhull drifted feverishly in and out of consciousness, no one was certain she would live. The newspapers, in mixed choruses of sorrow and skepticism, either announced that she was on the brink of death or speculated that this was another Woodhull humbug.

When the long-delayed obscenity trial against the *Weekly* was at last heard on June 26, 1873, Woodhull was weak and enervated by the heat, fanning herself with her hat in the courtroom. To her great relief, the judge agreed that at the time of the *Weekly*'s special edition no law prohibited obscenity in newspapers, and he instructed the jury to find the defendant not guilty. Eight months after Comstock had mounted the charge, the obscenity case was dismissed. Luther Challis's libel case remained to be settled.

Woodhull returned to the lecture circuit, first, as the financial crisis of September 1873 erupted in New York, to themes about power invested in the hands of the rich. Her second, more spectacular, lecture broke new ground, with a text she entitled apocalyptically "Tried As By Fire." By her own reckoning, she addressed this lecture to more than a quarter of a million people in 150 appearances in cities and towns all across the country. It was one of her most successful lectures—simple, lyrical, and delivered with her familiar passionate earnestness, a lecture not inflated with the pedantry of Stephen Pearl Andrews, who had withdrawn from Woodhull's inner circle.

In "Tried As By Fire," Woodhull spoke about human sexuality with a frankness seldom heard before in such public meetings. As she stood before her audiences, a beautiful woman in a black dress with a white rose at her throat, her unselfconscious candor was compelling. She urged that an interest in the welfare of humanity must prevail in the most intimate affairs of human beings. Earlier, Woodhull had argued for sexual freedom in the tradition of human rights as they were declared during the American Revolution. In "Tried As By Fire," she appropriated the familiar 19th-century feminine ideals of virtue and purity and linked them to the right of sexual self-determination. Owning and controlling one's own body "is what it means to be virtuous," she told her audiences, and "what it means to be pure." This

THE LIVING DEATH OF A MOTHER

In her popular lecture tour "Tried As By Fire," delivered across the country in 1874, Victoria Woodhull argued that healthy children could only be produced from healthy parents who loved each other. Condemning marriage based on legal necessity or economic dependence, Woodhull disclosed to audiences the impaired condition of her son Byron, whose profound retardation she blamed on her own unhappy marriage as a girl to the alcoholic Canning Woodhull.

My sisters. Oh! What shall I say to them; how awaken them to realize the awful responsibilities conferred through their maternal functions . . . Oh! Mothers, that I could make you feel these things as I know them. I do not appeal to you as a novice, ignorant of what I speak, merely to excite your sympathies, but as one having learned through long years of bitter experience. . . . Go home with me and see desolation and devastation in another form. The cold, iron bolt has entered my heart and left my life a blank, in ashes upon my lips. Wherever I go I carry a living corpse in my breast, the vacant stare of whose living counterpart meets me at the door of my home. My boy, now nineteen years of age, who should have been my pride and my joy, has never been blessed by the dawning of reasoning. I was married at fourteen, ignorant of everything that related to my maternal functions. For this ignorance, and because I knew no better than to surrender my maternal functions to a drunken man, I am cursed with this living death. Do you think my mother's heart does not yearn for the love of my boy? Do you think I do not realize the awful condition to which I have consigned him? Do you think I would not willingly give my life to make him what he has a right to be? Do you think his face is not ever before me pressing me on to declare these

continued on next page

continued from previous page

terrible social laws to the world? Do you think with this sorrow seated on my soul I can ever sit quietly down and permit women to go on ignorantly repeating my crime? Do you think I can ever cease to hurl the bitterest imprecations against the accursed thing that has made my life one long misery? Do you think I can ever hesitate to warn the young maidens against my fate, or to advise them never to surrender the control of their maternal functions to any man! Ah! If you do, you do not know the agony that rests here. Not to do less than I am doing were madness; it were worse than crime; it were the essence of ten thousand crimes concentrated in one soul to sink it in eternal infamy.

TRIED AS BY FIRE;

OR,

THE TRUE AND THE FALSE,

SOCIALLY.

AN ORATION DELIVERED BY

VICTORIA C. WOODHULL,

IN ALL

The Principal Cities and Towns of the Country during an engagement of

ONE HUNDRED AND FIFTY CONSECUTIVE NIGHTS,

TO AUDIENCES TOGETHER NUMBERING

A QUARTER OF A MILLION OF PEOPLE.

New York:
WOODHULL & CLAFLIN.
1874.

new feminine ideal of autonomy, she argued, would perfect human society.

Woodhull's theories of the science of human reproduction had long been brewing. Although she had blamed her son Byron's mental retardation on the state of her early marriage to the alcoholic Canning Woodhull, she had never before disclosed this personal history to an audience. Now she offered her beliefs in the transmission of birth defects as a science of reproduction. Simply put, she explained to her audiences, "Women cannot bear their best children except by the men they love best and for whom they have the keenest desire." "Because I knew no better than to surrender my maternal functions to a drunken man," she said, remembering Canning Woodhull and then alluding to Byron, "I am cursed with this living death."

Woodhull's understanding of inheritable traits in human reproduction was more fanciful than scientific. But her claims gave a new urgency to the argument that the institution of marriage, based on the economic and legal dependence of women, should end. Woodhull was not only arguing that forced submission to sexual relations in marriage was a form of human slavery. She was now insisting that such submission endangered the propagation of a healthy human species.

Woodhull was also confirming a new right to say "yes" as well as "no," a right that defied the longstanding nineteenth-century notion that virtuous women were incapable of sexual pleasure. The same utopian hopes that condemned forced relations in marriages based on economy, not love, also encouraged women to understand and accept the pleasure of their own bodies when they did love. With such autonomy and self-ownership in place, Woodhull imagined "no more sickness, no more poverty, no more crime." Instead, she envisioned "peace, plenty, and security, health, purity and virtue." With her few brave words, she was forcing into the light of public life a conversation about a subject that had long lain in ignorance.

On March 13, 1874, Woodhull appeared in court to hear the disposition of the Challis libel case against her. Almost a year and a half had passed since the arresting officers had first come to the office on Bond Street. When at last the jury declared Woodhull not guilty, the *Herald* reported that Annie Claflin blessed them joyously, while Woodhull and Tennie wept. But the long journey through the court system had left Victoria Woodhull altered. She was not able to sustain another blow to her pride when a disaffected supporter, Dr. Joseph Treat, a medical doctor and spiritualist, suddenly turned against her. In the past Woodhull had returned insult for insult, but Treat's barrage of abuse wearied her. Treat published bitterly cruel pamphlets, calling her a "harlot" and defaming every female member of her family, including her young daughter Zulu and the aged Annie Claflin. The press gleefully took up the new accusations and began a new campaign of invective against the "satanic" Mrs. Woodhull.

Meanwhile, the accusations Victoria Woodhull had made against the Reverend Henry Ward Beecher were being resurrected by none other than his former protégé and admirer Theodore Tilton. For five months in the new year 1875, the newspaper-reading public across the nation was enthralled by charges Tilton pressed in civil court against Beecher, whom he accused of adultery with his wife. Tilton had kept his grievance against Beecher silent for several years after he first claimed to have pried a confession from his wife Elizabeth. Privately, Tilton had hoped that in return for his silence Beecher would assist him in finding favor again with his former employer Henry Bowen, a wealthy Plymouth Church congregant. Bowen had hired Tilton as editor of the Brooklyn newspaper *The Independent,* but had subsequently fired him as his own social and religious views became more conservative and Tilton's advocacy of more liberal divorce laws in New York began to offend both Bowen and his newspaper's readers.

To keep the gossip quiet, Tilton had befriended Victoria Woodhull in 1871, hoping to convince her to refrain from naming Beecher an adulterer.

In the intervening years, Tilton and Beecher's apparent agreement to keep silent about the threatening scandal broke apart. In 1874 Tilton published a note from Beecher in which the minister apologized to Tilton for an offense he did not name and said he wished he were dead; Tilton understood the note as a confession of adultery. Beecher responded to Tilton's revelation by asking Plymouth Church to investigate the charges, suggesting six stalwart Beecher friends for the panel. In the church hearing that followed, Tilton accused Beecher of adultery with his wife, but no one was surprised when the panel acquitted Beecher of all charges and expelled Tilton from the church. "We find nothing in evidence," claimed the church panel, "that should impair the perfect confidence of Plymouth Church or the world in the Christian character and integrity of Henry Ward Beecher."

Enraged by the expulsion and the unwavering support Beecher had been able to win, Tilton filed a civil suit against his former friend in Brooklyn city court in January 1875, and the scandal exploded into open sessions. In court, Elizabeth Tilton claimed that a confession she had given to her husband had been elicited under duress. To soil Tilton's character further, Beecher's defense lawyer called Victoria Woodhull to the stand to place into evidence a few notes Tilton had written to her during the summer of their friendship. The notes suggested no intimacy, but, in the aftermath of the obscenity charges of 1872 and 1873, any association with the notorious Victoria Woodhull was sufficient to damage a reputation. The *Herald* reported that Beecher, when called to give testimony, described Woodhull as at the center of "loathsome scandals . . . with a greedy and unclean appetite for everything that was foul and vile."

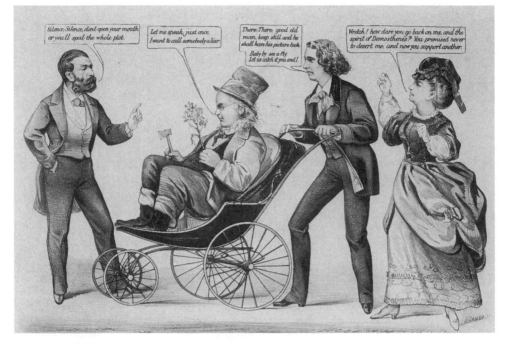

Victoria Woodhull, walking behind her former supporter Theodore Tilton, reproaches him for abandoning her Presidential campaign in favor of publisher Horace Greeley (in the baby carriage). Greeley's breakaway Republican party also gained the support of Democratic party chairman August Belmont (on the left).

After long months of testimony, the court trial ended in a hung jury. The popular Brooklyn minister emerged, apparently unharmed by the scandals, to ascend his pulpit at Plymouth Church. Beecher's church had raised $100,000 for his legal fees and published his defense lawyer's summations for distribution to libraries across the country. With few resources at his disposal to tell his side of the story, the embarrassed and discredited Theodore Tilton lived out the remainder of his life in Europe, his career as a lecturer and journalist in the United States ended. Elizabeth Tilton, living with her daughter in New Jersey, briefly re-emerged from obscurity in 1878 when she once again changed her story, this time writing a letter to newspapers saying that Beecher had indeed been her lover.

The scandal also hurt the suffrage movement. From the witness stand, Beecher had called Woodhull's suffragist friends "human hyenas." He said his sister Isabella Beecher Hooker was insane. For six months the newspapers had served up verbatim copy of lawyers mocking all reformers, all women's rights advocates. One *Herald* editorial proclaimed that "Thirty years of agitation in favor of woman suffrage ends in the triumph of a flock of ravens to pick the carcass of Henry Ward Beecher and croak the doctrine of home, marriage, love, motherhood, and religion." The collapse of the Tilton marriage and the threat to the Beechers' seemed to vindicate the dire warnings of those who opposed reform, as both liberal ministries such as Beecher's and reform opinions such as Tilton's did not seem to support stable homes.

As for Victoria Woodhull, the woman who had appeared in court to give testimony in the Beecher trial had seemed vastly different from the "terrible siren" of the popular press. She had dressed decorously in a black suit, hat, and veil. There was no rose at her throat as when she strode forth defiantly in public assemblies to declare war against hypocrisy, injustice, and forces leagued against women's freedom. The *Herald* reported that she was hesitant, her hands trembled, her face reddened when she spoke, apparently unsure of what precisely to say. Anyone sitting in court that day might have recognized that Victoria Woodhull was losing confidence.

Illness, exhaustion, and public ridicule had weakened her, drained her of her capacity to rally and of the will to defend the most radical ideas about economic, political, and personal freedom that had filled the assemblies where she spoke. Although her most steadfast adversary, Anthony Comstock, lost his court battle against Woodhull, the old crusader against vice may have claimed the final victory. The persecution he launched ultimately persuaded Victoria Woodhull to sanitize and disarm her arguments for sexual autonomy. Beginning her lectures with readings from the scriptures, she made free love look more respectable, less distinguishable from religious faith. "God is love and love is God," she lectured in Boston. At the same time, in the several years that followed her acquittal in court, she silenced her democratic appeal for labor and land reform, and abandoned the work for woman suffrage that had begun her public life.

Woodhull's brokerage had failed, her friends on Wall Street and in the suffrage movement had withdrawn. She felt hounded, persecuted, brought to bay, and increasingly friendless. She had known poverty from childhood and learned early that she must depend wholly on herself to thrive. But she was not made, she wrote in the *Weekly* "of flinty stuff." The "deluges of filth that are poured upon me," she complained, had worn her out. The Victoria Woodhull who emerged from the scathing personal attacks, arrests, and imprisonments returned to the model of her prairie childhood, Bible in hand, seeking revelations and offering inspirations. She spoke to audiences of a respectable size, but no longer to overflowing crowds with people standing in the rear of the hall. She had not lost her appeal to audiences, but she called these "weary years," and indeed, it seemed as though she were gradually withdrawing from the life she had built.

"Public Opinion," represented in Roman garb, recoils from Victoria Woodhull after she broke open the Beecher-Tilton scandal. She described herself as "the scapegoat . . . offered up as a victim to society by those who cover over the foulness of their lives."

Choosing not to attend the annual convention of the fractious American Association of Spiritualists, which had been quarreling over their support for her, Woodhull relinquished its presidency. In 1876 she published the last issue of the *Weekly,* which had been losing ground. Reflecting her own personal alterations, the *Weekly* had featured fewer articles crusading for social and economic justice and more articles that reflected

Woodhull's religious speculations. A few months later, Woodhull divorced Colonel Blood. For ten years, Blood had been her business associate and companion, but they found themselves now without the shared interest in political reform that had kept their companionable marriage strong.

Left to her were her sisters, her parents, and her children, the same Claflin flock who had accompanied her to New York City when she first set out to make her fortune on Wall Street. Although that money was long lost, Woodhull still had the proceeds of her successful lecture tour. More money may have come her way from an unexpected source. When Cornelius Vanderbilt died in 1877, he left most of his fortune to his son William, whose siblings contested the will, charging their father was senile when he signed it. William Vanderbilt, the heir, worried that Woodhull and Claflin might be called to court to testify about his father's interest in spiritualism, an interest the court might interpret as evidence of senility. Rumors circulated that William gave Woodhull and Claflin a generous settlement if they would leave town in advance of a summons to court.

The sisters left the country. In the warm summer when, at the peak of her success, Woodhull had shared her childhood memories with Theodore Tilton, she had told him that there was something in the name "Victoria" that forbade the very thought of failure. She had her voice, her stage presence, an indomitable will, and cash in her pocket. In August 1877, Woodhull took her family to England to start all over again.

7

SAFE HARBOR: THE SECOND CAREER OF VICTORIA WOODHULL

I was pleased to hear from your sister that your domestic trials have ended so happily and that you were in a safe harbor at last.
—Elizabeth Cady Stanton to Victoria Woodhull, Novmber 1, 1886

Many years later, as an old woman living out her years on a country estate in England, Woodhull wrote, "I gave America my youth. It was sweet and gallant and fruitful." As she reminisced, she seems not to have regretted the tempests and terrors of the first half of her life. Yet she did not hesitate to alter her own history as she shaped a new life across the Atlantic. She was nearly 40 years old when she arrived in England, not always in good health, uncertain how she would live, with Zulu, Byron, and an aged mother depending upon her. At first she made overtures to the British woman suffrage movement. When suffragist leader Millicent Fawcett made inquiries about her, Susan B. Anthony advised her to keep Woodhull at arm's length. "Both sisters are regarded as lewd and indecent," she wrote to Fawcett.

It seemed to Victoria Woodhull that she could not cast off the disabling and damaged reputation that clung to her from the Beecher trials. She had indeed preached free love, but she was neither lewd nor indecent. When Elizabeth Tilton wrote her confessional letter to the newspapers in 1878, English newspapers carried the story of Woodhull as the notorious woman behind the scandal. Desperate to establish herself, Woodhull continued the transformation she had begun at home. She became conventional.

Few who remembered the jaunty Alpine hat, mannish jackets, and short loose curls she had sported earlier would have recognized the new Victoria Woodhull. For the lecture tour she had arranged to give in England, Woodhull wore sober ruffled dresses with lace shawls, her long hair decorously gathered at her neck. She also made more palatable the arguments she uttered from English podiums, as she abandoned her most radical opinions.

As Woodhull settled in England, she adopted theories of eugenics, the name given by early social scientists to principles of selective breeding aimed at producing an improved human race. Although eugenics has now been discredited, such theories enjoyed widespread currency in the late decades of the 19th century and well into the 20th century. After Adolf Hitler adopted selective breeding in his design for a master race of Aryan peoples, eugenics was laid to rest, exposed as pseudoscience serving an elitism that justified genocide. But in the 1880s, Victoria Woodhull and many other progressive social thinkers found the principles of eugenics appealing as a scientific approach to human affairs, an application of the fairly new survival-of-the-fittest doctrines of biologist Charles Darwin.

Drawing less on religion now and more on Darwin, Woodhull was able to elaborate familiar themes for education about sexuality. "The mothers are incapable of teaching their children what they themselves have not been taught," she told audiences in a lecture called "Stirpiculture" and subtitled "The Scientific Propagation of the Human Race." In the interests of selective breeding, she was able to suggest as well the virtues of a planned parenthood. "The more intelligent the individuals," she argued in a lecture called "The Multiplication of the Unfit," "the more they think of consequences and the less likely are they to be influenced by sexual passion alone." In "Tried As By Fire," she had disclosed to American audiences her enduring sadness that her son Byron was so damaged. In England, her girlhood marriage to the drunken Canning Woodhull could not have been far from her mind when she told audiences "Go anywhere among the most miserable of any community, and you will find there the largest number of improvident marriages. Mere girls and boys, married and not married, become parents before complete maturity."

When her first lecture series opened in London, reviews were favorable, although some reports of the American scandals had already crossed the Atlantic and raised questions about her past. Still, wrote one reviewer, "Her half-nervous style of utterance, her little womanly ways, so out of keeping with the matter of her lecture, pleased the audience." One man who had come to hear her in London fell in love with her, and, after some years of calming his own misgivings and those of his family, he married her.

John Biddulph Martin was the heir of a wealthy, socially prominent, and long-established London banking family. To win the approval of the Martins, Woodhull completed the reinvention of her past, giving herself illustrious ancestors and recasting her scoundrel father Buck, who had followed her to London, as a sage and gentlemanly lawyer. She altered the spelling of her last name from Woodhull to Woodhall to distance herself from her notorious past. In a similar spirit of orthographic reinvention, her daughter Zulu became Zula.

What was more distressing to those who admired her courage at home, in 1881 she published a special single edition of the *Weekly* in which she denied that she had ever espoused free love, claiming that Andrews and Blood had authored arguments printed under her name while she was

busy miles away on lecture tours. In the years that followed, she would protest again and again that she had not uttered the words in Steinway Hall insisting on the human right to love whenever and as often as one pleased. "Free love is not what I ask for nor what I pleaded for," she wrote in a journal she began publishing in 1892, the *Humanitarian*. "What I asked for was educated love that one's daughters be taught to love rightly."

As Mrs. Martin, Victoria Woodhull accompanied her husband to the opera, gave dinner parties, and traveled abroad to collect treasures for their London mansion in Hyde Park Gate. To complete the storybook transformation of the Claflin sisters, Tennie, who had come to England with Woodhull, met and married Francis Cook, a wealthy manufacturer. When Cook became a baronet, Tennie became Lady Cook, a member of the aristocracy. Years later, Tennie arranged the presentation of one of Annie Claflin's great-granddaughters to Queen Victoria, after whom Woodhull had been named.

Victoria Woodhull and her third husband, John Biddulph Martin, called their imposing red-brick Victorian mansion "a dear nest." Martin wrote later of his love for Woodhull, "When you were with her everything became so thrilling, so worthwhile."

The Martins' marriage was happy, and some of Woodhull's old companions among the suffragists, such as Stanton, who had been sympathetic to her in misfortune, rejoiced that she had landed safely. Woodhull was again a wealthy woman, but she was no more willing to retire into comfortable obscurity than she had been years earlier when she won her fortune on Wall Street. As Mrs. John Martin, Woodhull became a philanthropic woman of letters, an English matron interested in the welfare of women and children and in applying scientific principles to agriculture and social institutions.

There were brief efforts to rekindle some of the more brilliant moments of her American career when she had ascended to the political stage as a Presidential hopeful almost a quarter-century earlier. With John Martin, she returned to the United States in 1892 to announce her candidacy for the next Presidential election. The Kansas delegation of a new National Equal Rights Party rallied to her side, and she began issuing the *Humanitarian, a Monthly Magazine of Sociology* in New York and London as if to reprise the *Weekly* as a sounding board for her campaign. It seemed she might resume her public life in America, but when she launched a lecture tour in New York two years later, the old fire was gone—no more spontaneous outbursts or striding back and forth across the stage and raising an arm as if to lead the audience into battle. The Martins returned to England.

Some unpleasantness arose in 1894. When the Martins discovered that the British Museum library

The six-pointed star engraved on Woodhull's personal stationery bears the letters of "kismet," meaning fate or destiny. This device recalled Woodhull's spiritualist conviction that true love, which she found with John Martin, is divinely intended.

housed pamphlets about the Beecher-Tilton scandals that described Woodhull as a blackmailer and prostitute, they sued the museum for libel. On the witness stand for two days, Woodhull was cross-examined lengthily about her American career as an actress, clairvoyant, medical healer, and spiritualist, as well as about her life as a reformer and suffragist. She was reminded of her avowal of free love in Steinway Hall, to which she responded with spirit that "Women are struggling for their freedom from sexual slavery" and the day would come when they would judge men's purity publicly as men now did women's. The Martin banking family and the British Museum were both important British institutions. The tactful verdict, allowing both sides to feel vindicated, supported the charge of libel and awarded the Martins a pittance in damages, but required them to pay the costs of the museum's defense.

Woodhull continued publication of the *Humanitarian* for several years after John Martin's death in 1897, writing more than 100 articles on a wide range of subjects from horticulture to poetry. She had not lost any of her passion for innovation, although she had abandoned the more dangerous challenges to social institutions that had brought her fame and infamy in the United States. She learned to use the typewriter, the bicycle, and the automobile, which she liked to drive at great speeds. When her London neighbor Sir Leslie Stephen, father of the author Virginia Woolf, wrote her a note complaining that driving automobiles was unladylike, she replied politely, but did not yield the wheel of her motor car. Later, as an old woman confined to English village life, she gave generously to charities, establishing schools for children and women. One afternoon she even entertained King Edward VII for tea when he came into her neighborhood. She had come a long way from her frontier childhood, but in a whimsical moment she named two cottages on the Martin family estate "Homer" and "Ohio," after her birthplace.

Victoria Woodhull lived long enough to see the vote finally granted to women in England and the United States, after the end of World War I. But the woman suffrage movement she had helped to invigorate wrote her out of their history. When Anthony, Stanton, and the suffragist Millicent Gage wrote the official account of their campaign in 1882, they offered only perfunctory mention of Woodhull's important Memorial to Congress, and failed to acknowledge her history-making Presidential candidacy, her brave arguments for the reform of marriage and divorce, and her courageous exposure of the moral hypocrisy of civic and religious leaders in post–Civil War America.

Woodhull died quietly in her sleep on June 9, 1927, having lived almost to her ninetieth year. In her will, she provided for the care of her son Byron, whom she had kept by her side since she had become a mother at fifteen, and left her great wealth to Zula, whom she hoped would write her biography. The obituary that ran in the *New York Times* praised Mrs. Martin as a suffrage advocate whose work had been largely forgotten by a younger generation of activists. But the newspapers were silent about her earlier confinements in the Ludlow Street jail and the Tombs. There was no speculation that she had been the victim of a shameful repression of free speech.

Woodhull had tried several times in retirement to tell the story of her life, but never got beyond a few sketchy notes. Having remade her own life so frequently, in the end she could not tell its story as one continuous and coherent tale. Nor was Zula able to fulfill the task. She had been badly shaken by an unflattering biography of Woodhull written by Emanie Sachs in 1928, the year after her mother's death. It seemed that the verdict on Victoria Woodhull as an uneducated, unscrupulous, and indecent woman must stand. After Zula died in 1940, trustees of her estate considered authorizing a biography, but concluded that publication would only bring the familiar sludge of Woodhull's detrac-

tors to the surface again. It remained for another generation of historians to tell Victoria Woodhull's story with the seriousness and tolerance her life deserved.

Among her nearer contemporaries, though, some admirers began her vindication. One young American lawyer, Marilla M. Ricker, writing to Victoria Woodhull Martin in London in 1905, coined the phrases with which to remember her: "Your work started it all. You gave women the idea that they must own themselves."

Woodhull had managed all of this in just a few years. With the suddenness of a firestorm she entered the national stage from America's heartland at the age of 32, a woman who embodied in herself the restless social mobility of post–Civil War America and its dynamic controversies. In her pilgrimage from the Midwest to the Pacific gold coast and back again, she had absorbed the political, social, and religious ferment of the years in which America trans-

Victoria Woodhull, driving her son Byron and her daughter Zula Maud, was enamored of automobiles. She liked to drive at the highest possible speeds and told friends she had given King Edward VII his first automobile ride when he visited her at her country estate.

141

formed itself from a rural agrarian republic to an urban industrial nation. In barely seven years on the American national stage, she represented various movements—spiritualism, socialism, feminism—in the passionate oratory of American democracy. She was convinced of her own value, insisting on her own rights and on the rights of the laboring classes from which she had come. Most of all, by being uncompromising about the rights of her sex, she forged her own legacy. To those who knew her, Victoria Woodhull was either martyr or demon, saint or trickster, a colorful and paradoxical woman who entered and shaped a national debate about human rights that continues into our own time.

"The Spirit to Run" is the legend on a T-shirt bearing her portrait, offered by a Victoria Woodhull website (www.victoria-woodhull.com) to celebrate her 1872 campaign. Another frontier, cyberspace has been colonized by a new wave of Woodhull admirers. With editions of the *Weekly* posted on the site, how pleased Woodhull would have been that the curtain has not rung down on her history-making performances.

CHRONOLOGY

September 23, 1838
Born in Homer, Ohio

January 24, 1848
Gold strike in California

November 23, 1853
Marries Canning Woodhull in Cleveland, Ohio

December 31, 1854
Gives birth to Byron Woodhull

1858
Moves family to San Francisco; Works as an actress

April 12, 1861
Civil War begins when Confederate troops fire on Union
soldiers at Fort Sumter, South Carolina

April 23, 1861
Gives birth to Zulu Maud Woodhull in New York

1864
Meets Colonel James Harvey Blood in St. Louis, Missouri

1865
Divorces Canning Woodhull in Chicago

July 12, 1866
Marries Colonel Blood in Dayton, Ohio

1868
Moves with Colonel Blood and various Claflins to 17 Great
Jones Street in New York City; Meets shipping tycoon and
financier Cornelius Vanderbilt

January 19, 1869
Attends National Convention of Woman Suffrage in
Washington, D.C.

September 24, 1869
Makes fortune on Wall Street on "Black Friday"

January 20, 1870

Opens stockbrokerage house of Woodhull, Claflin and Co. on Wall Street

April 2, 1870

Announces her candidacy for the U.S. Presidency

April 5, 1870

Moves into mansion on 38th Street in New York City

May, 1870

Meets Stephen Pearl Andrews, utopian reformer

May 21, 1870

Publishes first edition of *Woodhull & Claflin's Weekly*

January 11, 1871

Presents Memorial (petition) on suffrage to House Judiciary Committee in Washington, D.C.

February 16, 1871

Lectures "On Constitutional Equality" in Washington, D.C.

May 8, 1871

Lectures on "The Great Social Problems of Labor and Capital" in New York City

May 15, 1871

Annie Claflin brings suit against Colonel Blood in New York

May 22, 1871

Meets Theodore Tilton, social reformer

July 4, 1871

Publishes call for Equal Rights Party

August 3, 1871

Delivers "A Speech on the Principles of Finance"

September 9, 1871

Becomes president of American Association of Spiritualists

November 7, 1871

Attempts to vote in New York City

November 20, 1871

Lectures on "The Principles of Social Freedom" in New York City

December, 1871
Assumes leadership of Section 12 of International Workingmen's
Association in New York City

January 10, 1872
Nominated for the U.S. Presidency by National Woman
Suffrage Convention in Washington

February 20, 1872
Lectures on "The Impending Revolution" in New York City

April 7, 1872
Canning Woodhull dies in New York

May 10, 1872
Nominated for the U.S. Presidency by Equal Rights Party in
New York

October 28, 1872
Publishes revelations about Henry Ward Beecher in the *Weekly*

November 2, 1872
Arrested with Tennessee Claflin in New York for violation of
Comstock laws

November 5, 1872
Ulysses S. Grant is reelected President of the United States

November 8, 1872
Luther Challis's libel charges added to Comstock indictment

January 9, 1873
Lectures on "The Naked Truth" in New York City; arrested at
conclusion of lecture

May 17, 1873
Brokerage firm of Woodhull, Claflin and Co. dissolved

June, 1873
Falls ill and recovers

June 26, 1873
Obscenity trial begins; charges are withdrawn

September 18, 1873
Financial markets collapse in New York

October 17, 1873
Lectures on "Reform or Revolution, Which?" in New York
City

1874
Begins countrywide lecture tour, "Tried As By Fire"

March 13, 1874
Acquitted of Challis's libel charge

August 1874
Joseph Treat publishes pamphlets defaming Woodhull

January 11, 1875
Theodore Tilton brings suit against Henry Ward Beecher in Brooklyn city court

July 2, 1875
Beecher-Tilton trial ends in hung jury

June 1876
Ceases publication of *Weekly*

October 6, 1876
Divorces Colonel Blood

August, 1877
Departs United States for England

1881
Publishes special edition of *Weekly*, repudiating radical social opinions

October 31, 1883
Marries John Biddulph Martin in London

July 1892
Publishes *The Humanitarian, a Monthly Magazine of Sociology*

September 22, 1892
Nominated for U.S. Presidency by Kansas delegation of Equal Rights Party

1893
Lectures on "The Scientific Propagation of the Human Race" in New York City and London

February 24, 1894
Brings suit against British Museum for libel

March 20, 1897
John Martin dies in Canary Islands

June 10, 1927
Dies in England at the age of 89

FURTHER READING

WRITINGS OF VICTORIA WOODHULL

Stern, Madeleine B., ed. *The Victoria Woodhull Reader.* Weston,
Mass.: M&S, 1974.
*This unpaginated compilation of Woodhull's major public addresses,
organized by subject matter, includes facsimile reproductions of reprints
from Woodhull and Claflin's Weekly. Includes analytical and
biographical introductions by the editor.*
Woodhull and Claflin's Weekly, May 14, 1870–June 10, 1876.
*Publication suspended some months in 1872; a special edition printed
in 1881.*

BIOGRAPHIES OF VICTORIA WOODHULL

Gabriel, Mary. *Notorious Victoria. The Life of Victoria Woodhull
Uncensored.* Chapel Hill: Algonquin, 1998.
Goldsmith, Barbara. *Other Powers: The Age of Suffrage, Spiritualism
and the Scandalous Victoria Woodhull.* New York: Harper
Perennial, 1988.
Marberry, M. Marion. *Vicky: A Biography of Victoria Woodhull.* New
York: Funk and Wagnalls, 1967.
Sachs, Emanie. *The Terrible Siren: Victoria Woodhull.* 1928. Reprint,
New York: Arno, 1978.
Tilton, Theodore. *Victoria C. Woodhull, A Biographical Sketch: Mr.
Tilton's Account of Mrs. Woodhull.* New York: The Golden Age,
1871.
Underhill, Lois Beachy. *The Woman Who Ran for President.* New
York: Penguin, 1995.

BIOGRAPHIES, CORRESPONDENCE, AND DIARIES
OF 19TH-CENTURY WOMEN'S RIGHTS LEADERS

Barry, Kathleen. *Susan B. Anthony: A Biography of a Singular
Feminist.* New York: New York University Press, 1988.
Carden, Elizabeth. *Antoinette Brown Blackwell, A Biography.* Old
Westbury, N.Y.: Feminist Press, 1983.
DuBois, Ellen, ed. *The Elizabeth Cady Stanton–Susan B. Anthony
Reader: Correspondence, Writings, Speeches.* Boston: Northeastern
University Press, 1992.
Gordon, Ann, ed. *Selected Papers of Elizabeth Cady Stanton and
Susan B. Anthony.* New Brunswick, N.J.: Rutgers University
Press, 2000.
Kerr, Andrea Moore. *Lucy Stone: Speaking Out for Equality.* New
Brunswick N.J.: Rutgers University Press, 1990.

Kolmerton, Carol A. *The American Life of Ernestine Rose.* Syracuse: Syracuse University Press, 1999.

Lasser, Carol, and Marlene Deahi Merrill, eds. *Friends and Sisters: Letters Between Lucy Stone and Antoinette Brown Blackwell, 1846–93.* Urbana: University of Illinois Press, 1987.

Lerner, Gerda. *The Grimké sisters from South Carolina: Rebels Against Slavery.* Boston: Houghton Mifflin, 1967.

Sherr, Lynn, ed. *Failure is Impossible: Susan B. Anthony in Her Own Words.* New York: Times Books, 1995.

Sigerman, Harriet. *Elizabeth Cady Stanton: The Right is Ours.* New York: Oxford University Press, 2001.

AMERICAN WOMEN IN THE 19TH CENTURY

Braude, Ann. *Radical Spirits: Spiritualism and Women's Rights in Nineteenth-Century America.* Boston: Beacon, 1989.

DuBois, Ellen. *Feminism and Suffrage: The Emergence of an Independent Women's Movement in America.* Ithaca, N.Y.: Cornell University Press, 1978.

Ehrenreich, Barbara, and Deirdre English. *For Her Own Good: 150 Years of the Experts' Advice to Women.* Garden City, New York: Anchor, 1978.

Flexner, Eleanor, and Ellen Fitzpatrick. *Century of Struggle: The Woman's Rights Movement in the United States.* Enl. edition. Cambridge, Mass.: Harvard University Press, 1996.

Gurko, Miriam. *The Ladies of Seneca Falls: The Birth of the Woman's Rights Movement.* New York: Schoken, 1974.

Horowitz, Helen Lefkowitz. *Rereading Sex: Battles over Sexual Knowledge and Suppression in Nineteenth-Century America.* New York: Knopf, 2002.

Ryan, Mary P. *Women In Public: Between Banners and Ballots, 1825–1880.* Baltimore: Johns Hopkins University Press, 1990.

Sigerman, Harriet. *Laborers for Liberty: American Women 1865–1890.* New York: Oxford University Press, 1994.

——. *An Unfinished Battle: American Women 1848–1865.* New York: Oxford University Press, 1994.

Smith, Karen Manners. *New Paths to Power: American Women 1890–1920.* New York: Oxford University Press, 1990.

Smith-Rosenberg, Carroll. *Disorderly Conduct: Visions of Gender in Victorian America.* New York: Oxford, 1985.

Wheeler, Marjorie Spruill. *New Women of the New South: The Leaders of the Woman Suffrage Movement in the Southern States.* New York: Oxford University Press, 1993.

INDEX

149

ACKNOWLEDGMENTS

Victoria Woodhull left behind a rich trail of papers—correspondence to her and about her and a generous history in newsprint that chronicles the dramatic moments of her career. I have depended on the many private collections which house these papers. Among them, the collection at Southern Illinois University at Carbondale and the Beecher-Hooker project in Hartford, Connecticut have been notably helpful. Other correspondence helpful to me in writing is located in the Olympia Brown Collection in the Schlesinger Library at Radcliffe College, the Sophia Smith Collection at Smith College, the Alma Lutz Collection at the Huntington Library, the Gerrit Smith Collection at Syracuse University, and the collection of the New York Historical Society.

A new generation of sympathetic historians has offered studies of Victoria Woodhull for the twenty-first century. Among these biographies, I was helped particularly by Lois Beachy Underhill's *The Woman Who Ran for President*.

From the earliest inception of this project, I have relied on the guidance of Nancy Toff, Vice President and Editorial Director of the Young Adult Reference division of Oxford University Press. The excellent standards she has established make contributing to the series a challenge and a pleasure. Preparing this manuscript for publication, I was immensely assisted by the careful reading of Professor Ellen Carol Dubois of UCLA. Good friends, Glenn Altschuler, Catherine Penner, and Carol Kammen also read the manuscript and offered advice. Michael Kammen helpfully passed books and references my way and was generous with interest and encouragement. As the manuscript made its way to print, it was assisted and improved by copy editor Anna Eberhard Friedlander and project and photo editor, Janielle Keith.

Above all and as always, I am grateful to Isaac Kramnick for sharing the library study, the word processor, and so much more.

PICTURE CREDITS

TEXT CREDITS

p. 13: Theodore Tilton, *Victoria C. Woodhull, A Biographical Sketch: Mr. Tilton's Account of Mrs. Woodhull,* (New York: The Golden Age, 1871.) Microfilm. New Haven, Conn.: Research Publications, Inc., 1976 (History of Women; 3010), 4, 6–7.

p. 55: *New York Herald,* April 2, 1870, 8.

p. 70: Victoria Woodhull, "A Lecture on Constitutional Equality, Feb. 16, 1871." (New York: Woodhull and Claflin, 1871). As reprinted in *The Victoria Woodhull Reader,* ed. Madeleine B. Stern (Weston, Mass.: M&S Press, 1974), 31–32.

p. 80: Victoria Woodhull, "A Speech on the Principles of Social Freedom, Nov. 20, 1871." (New York: Woodhull and Claflin, 1871). As reprinted in *The Victoria Woodhull Reader,* ed. Madeleine B. Stern (Weston, Mass.: M&S Press, 1974), 15–16.

p. 99: Victoria Woodhull, "A Speech on the Impending Revolution," Feb. 1, 1872. (New York: Woodhull and Claflin, 1872). As reprinted in *The Victoria Woodhull Reader,* ed. Madeleine B. Stern (Weston, Mass.: M&S Press, 1974), 16–17.

p. 125: Victoria Woodhull, "Tried As By Fire, or the True and the False Socially." (New York: Woodhull and Claflin, 1874). As reprinted in *The Victoria Woodhull Reader,* ed. Madeleine B. Stern (Weston, Mass.: M&S Press, 1974), 26–27.

Miriam Brody is the editor of the Penguin Classics edition of Mary Wollstonecraft's *Vindication of the Rights of Woman* and the author of the Oxford Portrait's biography of Mary Wollstonecraft. She is also the author of *Manly Writing*, a study of gender and style in 18th-century schooltexts and in contemporary advice to writers. She is currently working on an edition of the autobiography of the Russian/Jewish anarchist Emma Goldman. Brody is a professor emeritus of the Department of Writing at Ithaca College.